PREFACE

For the greater part of the last fifty years, many war-time records have been hidden from public scrutiny but now, some of the secrets of the Second World War are gradually revealed to those who have the patience to delve amongst the historic documents. Most of these papers are with the Public Record Office but others are in private hands or in local Archives. My task in researching and collating detail of war-time activities in Anglesey, Caernarvonshire and Merionethshire, as the counties were at that time, has been a fascinating one. Unfortunately, it cannot possibly be a complete account because of difficulties in gaining access to some records. There are many excellent books written on various aspects of the war; mine is merely an attempt to collate and record extracts from records of war-time incidents and activity in Gwynedd together with personal recollections.

I am indebted to the Marquess of Anglesey for his time and guidance and for allowing me to delve amongst the private documents and papers at Plas Newydd. Much of the interesting detail concerning the work of the Anglesey War Agricultural Executive Committee was gleaned from those papers.

The Archivist and staff at Gwynedd Archives Service at Caernarvon and Llangefni have once again been most helpful and patient. I would also thank Mr Tomos Roberts of the Manuscript Department of the University College of North Wales Library for his assistance and guidance.

I am grateful to Dr Ian Hilton of the Department of Modern Languages, University College of North Wales for the translation of German letters and documents which he willingly undertook. Also my thanks to Mr W Alister Williams for undertaking the task of reading the manuscript and for his assistance and suggestions.

Mrs Mary K Murphy ALA, Archivist, Institution of Civil Engineers, London has been of considerable assistance with regard to information on H Iorys Hughes and the Mulberry Harbour.

My thanks also to Miss Jacqueline McComish, Research Assistant, National Gallery, London for allowing me access to material relating to the transfer and storing of pictures in North Wales.

Mr R E Roberts, Penmaenmawr has been most generous in providing many documents, photographs and newspaper cuttings etc. relating to the Royal Air Force, Observer Corps and the RAF Mountain Rescue Service.

I also wish to acknowledge the assistance which I have received from the following:

After the Battle magazine; Ministry of Defence, Air Historical Branch (RAF); Avro International Aerospace; British Aerospace Plc., Farnborough; British Broadcasting Corporation, Bangor; British Broadcasting Corporation, Cardiff; British Museum; Brooklands Museum Trust Ltd., Weybridge; Cambridge University Library; Clwyd County Council, Library and Information Service; Mr George Crabb; Miss Joan Davies; Mr John C Davies; Diamond Information Centre, London; Dulwich Preparatory College; Mr Dewi Ellis; Exposition Permanent Du Debarquement, Arromanches, Normandy, France; Mr John Hawley; Hunting Plc.; Hunting Aviation Ltd.; Imperial War Museum; Mr D Kay; Lancfile; Llyfrgell Gwynedd; Lloyds Bank Plc.; Mr Malcolm H D McAlpine, Sir Robert McAlpine Ltd.; Ministry of Defence, Air Historical Branch (RAF); Ministry of Defence, Chemical & Biological Defence Establishment; National Gallery, London; National Library of Wales; National Museum of Wales; Public Record Office; Prof. Dr. Jürgen Rohwer; Royal Air Force Association; Royal Air Force Museum,

Hendon; Mr H E Scrope; The Cha Institution of Civil Engineers; T Cuxhaven, Germany; Welsh Office; Wins, Antwerp; Women's Royal Voluntary Service Archives.

And last but certainly not least, the very many individuals who recounted personal recollections and experiences of the war and allowed me to make copies of photographs and memorabilia which had been carefully preserved through the intervening years.

Abbreviations used:
   BGP - Bangor General Papers (UCNW Archives)
   GAS - Gwynedd Archives Service (Caernarvon)
   PNP - Plas Newydd Papers
   PYR - Porth yr Aur Papers
   UCNW - University College of North Wales

All references to money are in the old, pre-decimalisation system of 12d being equal to 1s and 20s being equal to £1. The present 1p is equal to 2.4d.

Wherever possible every effort has been made to trace the copyright of the photographs used.

CHAPTER 1: Introduction

In the years leading up to the Second World War, opinions varied as to Hitler's intentions and eventual ambitions. His ability to tantalise the people of Germany appeared to extend to politicians of other countries. Following on a meeting arranged by Hitler at his country residence at Berchtesgaden in Germany in September 1936 with Lloyd George, the latter stated: "The idea of a Germany intimidating Europe with a threat that its irresistible army might march across frontiers form no part in the new vision".

Even though Hitler's intentions had become obvious by 1938, pleas for peace continued to be made by many countries including Britain with periodic visits by the Prime Minister, Neville Chamberlain to Munich. These visits came to nothing and the German war machine started to roll across Europe. In preparation for a war which seemed inevitable between Britain and Germany, Parliament voted in favour of conscription and it became necessary for men aged between 20 and 21 years of age on 3 June 1939, with certain exceptions, to register at a Ministry of Labour Employment Exchange under the Military Training Act 1939. [GAS XM6972/8]

The colossal waste of life and the horror inflicted on mind and body during the First World War was still indelibly imprinted on the memory of those who survived the carnage even though twenty years had elapsed. It was little wonder that pacifism and nationalism were advocated in the late 1930s. There were many demonstrations against conscription in Wales and when a crowd of about 1,000 attended an anti-conscription meeting conducted by a number of Free Church ministers at Pwllheli, the audience adopted – without dissent – a resolution declaring opposition to compulsory military training. The Rev. J W Jones, of Criccieth said that the conscription measure undermined the freedom of individuals and was a denial of the spirit of the Gospel. He also protested against the holding of Air Raid Precautions' displays and recruiting parades on Sundays. A similar rally was held on 27 May 1939:

"Mr W Oliver Brown of Glasgow will be among the speakers at the anti-conscription rally at the Caernarvon Eisteddfod Pavilion tomorrow. Mr Brown represents the Scottish Neutrality League a movement working for Scotland's neutrality in all wars...Also attending at the above meeting will be Richard Bishop of Dolgellau (Welsh Pacifist Society)" [C&DH 26.5.39]

However, not everyone was in agreement with pacifism as shown in the following letter:

> "Conscription has come and is long overdue. It is meeting with strong opposition from religious bodies in North Wales. The same thing happened on the eve of the last war...our cheery little band of Nationalists naturally object. They look forward to the day when Herr Hitler 'delivers them from the brutal English yoke'. But it would be well to remember that Herr Hitler has a poor sense of humour."
> [C&DH 2.6.39]

The first indication of the seriousness of the situation, especially to the youngsters who had not experienced the tragedy of the First World War, were the posters distributed around towns and villages in August 1939 advising where and when gas masks were to be issued. These hideous items were intended to be carried on the person from the start of hostilities. At the same time villages and towns in North Wales were told to prepare for an influx of evacuees from Merseyside and other areas which were expected to be affected by bombing raids. When the 'mothers and babies' evacuee contingent arrived during the first few days of September they were given temporary accommodation in local community halls, schools and chapel vestries until more permanent arrangements could be made. Centralised facilities including feeding and bedding, which had been in store since early 1939 in anticipation of such an eventuality, were organised by the Women's Voluntary Service (WVS).

Even after war had been declared the *Caernarvon and Denbigh Herald* stated on 8 September 1939:

> "Our leaders have stated that Great Britain has no quarrel with the German people. That is the truth. The British people have sought peace and friendly relations with the great nation but Hitler would not listen to appeals for conciliation. The Archbishop of Canterbury … says of Hitler that he is 'the last man to listen to peaceful persuasion'… This war is now called 'Hitler's War'…"

Details of every individual in the United Kingdom, except those in the armed forces were compiled by enumerators on Friday 29 September 1939, and used for the eventual National Register and the issue of ration books and identity cards, and replaced the scheduled 1941 census. Registration was compulsory and penalties were inflicted for non compliance or for giving false information (C&DH 22.9.39).

It would appear that during the first few weeks of the war not everyone had abandoned the possibility of peace:

> "On Oct. 3 on the floor of the House of Commons Mr Lloyd George made a most stirring speech on the international situation warning the Government not to come to a hasty decision when considering peace offers. The Speech, as was expected, was subjected to much criticism in some quarters …"

On 21 October 1939, Lloyd George (Liberal Member of Parliament for Caernarvon 1890-1944, Chancellor of the Exchequer, 1908-11, Prime Minister 1916-22) addressed an unexpectedly large audience estimated at between six and eight thousand on the subject 'Peace Aims' at Caernarvon Pavilion. He started his speech in Welsh and went on to deal with Munich and Chamberlain's approaches to Hitler. He said that he had been falsely accused of proposing surrender:

> "...I simply proposed a conference now before the great slaughter began and not years hence when millions of young men have been killed, perhaps also many women and children...A conference now to save the world from the miseries and uncertainties of a prolonged war and before the nations become exhausted and impoverished and civilisation had been thrown back decades. That was my proposal…"

Such was Lloyd George's reputation that, with Neville Chamberlain as Prime Minister and Winston Churchill, First Lord of the Admiralty, many of his admirers wondered why he had not been included in the War Cabinet:

> "… (he) is still full of vigour and a man possessing his outstanding abilities would be of invaluable help to the Government in the present situation … At 76 he may be too old for a strenuous executive post but his experience, his genius for disengaging essentials from 'red tape' and his superb confidence in a crisis would be invaluable in some advisory capacity." [C&DH Notes of the Week 15.9.39]

Chamberlain, however, was determined not to have Lloyd George in his cabinet although it is doubtful if the latter would have any such desire such was the contempt that he had for the Prime Minister whom he felt was the last person to lead the country through the war. Lloyd George was still very much an orator when he appeared on a public platform but such occasions were by then infrequent and appearances in the House of Commons left him in a tired state.

When Chamberlain was succeeded as Prime Minister by Winston Churchill in May 1940, the latter offered Lloyd George a position in the Ministry of Agriculture but it was declined because of his age (he had already celebrated fifty years as a Member of Parliament on 12 April 1940) and the fact that he had no desire to serve in any Government alongside Chamberlain.

Meanwhile, in Wales, attempts at procuring peace continued and a resolution was passed calling upon the Government to acquiesce to a truce and an international conference. It also stated that:

> "… Professor J E Daniel, President of the Welsh Nationalist Party... (is) to appeal to the Government immediately to take the initiative in securing an armistice and calling a conference to discuss a new European order…" [C&DH 13.10.39]

At a conference at Caernarvon on Saturday, the Rev. Lewis Valentine (the first president of the Welsh Nationalist Party) said that "… these days of war were of great danger to Wales". The Party's duty he said was to see that Wales did not cease to exist as a nation when England was supposed to be fighting for the justice of other small nations. The conference attitude to the war was reflected in two resolutions which were unanimously passed namely:

> "1. That this conference of the Welsh Nationalist Party firmly believing that nothing but evil can come to Wales through this war requests the Government to call an Armistice and peace conference without delay.
> 2. By accepting Welsh Nationality as sufficient grounds for conscience objections to military service..." [C&DH 27.10.39]

In an attempt to appease the situation, Mr Hore-Belisha as Secretary of State for War stated that the War Office was very conscious of the feeling in Wales and that those who governed such matters would be in favour of keeping a man in the unit of his choice.

The inconvenience of rationing of food, petrol, clothing and other material, was grudgingly accepted with periodic dissension. Perhaps the least inconvenienced by these wartime conditions were the poorer families whose ability to purchase was governed, not by rationing, but by lack of money.

Cars were still regarded as luxury items at the start of the war and available to only a few. Most were taken off the road and placed in store for the duration of hostilities because of the shortage of petrol and the difficulty in maintaining the vehicles. Petrol was only available to very few essential users such as doctors but even then it was severely rationed and became progressively more difficult to obtain.

With the German army poised on the Continent and the threat of invasion imminent in 1940, the Local Defence Volunteers (LDV), later to be called the Home Guard, were organised so that any man left in a town or village who had not been enlisted into the armed forces, was coerced into joining a motley crowd of defenders. They were dependent, at least in the critical part of the war, on using whatever weapon that came to hand, if it became necessary to repel invaders, and were dressed in a uniform which was limited to an armband bearing the initials LDV.

The threat of bombing and invasion, emphasised in many Government leaflets and pamphlets, was sufficient to ensure that everyone involved with Air Raid Precautions, Auxiliary Fire Service, Red Cross, St John's Ambulance, Women's Voluntary Service and other organisations undertook their duties very seriously.

On Wednesday 29 May 1940, the Government issued an instruction requesting the Divisional Road Engineer for Wales to remove at once

"... all direction signs on Public Highways throughout the County. Precedence should be given in the first instance to Trunk Roads and Classified Roads, attention to the Unclassified Roads following in due course. Action in the first instance should be confined to roads outside built-up areas...I should emphasise that the posts can remain for the ultimate replacement of the signs..."

The Women's Institute (WI) and Women's Voluntary Services carried out many services during the war including running small cafés for the benefit of local servicemen based at nearby camps or visiting seaports. These places were well patronised if only for a cup of tea poured out of a pot rather than out of metal urns into which mysterious and unwelcome ingredients were believed to have been added, at military establishments.

During the period when Liverpool, Manchester and other towns and cities in the north west were subjected to heavy bombing, the distinctive drone of the German planes as they passed overhead, would remind everyone of their vulnerability. Gwynedd was also subjected to some aerial attacks, but, fortunately, nothing like that which other places suffered.

CHAPTER 2: Civil Defence Services

The Munich crisis of 1938 was the catalyst for over a million men and women in the United Kingdom to join the Civil Defence or the ARP (Air Raid Precautions) as it was generally known. This multi-role army of civilians were responsible for trench digging in the larger towns and cities so as to give protection at the time of an air raid when other shelters were not at hand. In Caernarvon, enrolment in the various civil defence services had mixed levels of success. By March 1939, recruitment for the ARP exceeded the number required by 500 whereas the regular fire brigade showed a deficiency of 10 and the Auxiliary Fire Service a deficiency of 280. However, 760 men had enrolled as Special Constables against the establishment of 734. [C&DH 10.3.39]

When war was declared, the first task of the Government was to protect the general public as much as possible from the expected aerial bombing attacks. Since lights created by street lamps, houses and other sources in towns and villages throughout the country might guide bombers to their targets, it was decided that they had to be extinguished wherever the source. The first task of the Minister of Home Security, Rt. Hon. Sir John Anderson, in conjunction with the police, was the enforcement of lighting regulations, which were to become known as the 'Black Out'. These regulations declared that

no light whatsoever was to be allowed to be emitted from any building during hours of darkness. Some over zealous individuals resorted to extreme measures as shown in a newspaper report in April 1940:

"...Police Sergeant D M Hughes told the magistrates (at Caernarvon) that he had to extinguish an unobscured light in an office building by shooting it with a .22 rifle..."

A letter sent by the Clerk of the Gwyrfai Rural District Council to the County ARP Controller on 19 March 1940 complained of lights showing at RAF Llanberis when the village was attacked by "hostile planes", a reply from the Chief Constable stated that the RAF had authority to carry out work with lights showing but these were to be extinguished when purple and red warnings were issued.

Even vehicles were regulated in the amount of light being shown and this was achieved by limiting the size of side and rear lights to 2" diameter and also masking headlights. As an additional precaution, front and rear bumpers were invariably painted white. Buses and trains had blue-painted lamps inside and windows were covered up at night. Shops were not allowed to show any lights and, with this in mind, boards were placed at the entrance whereby shoppers entering during hours of darkness had to negotiate a zig-zag course. Pedestrians requiring to be out at night wore a white band on their clothing so as to make themselves more easily seen, particularly by vehicle drivers. Bands of white paint were painted on lamp posts and the edges of pavements were similarly painted as an aid to pedestrians at night. The end of British Summer Time was delayed until 19 November so as to extend daylight hours.

Llanfairisgaer Local Committee decided, like many other communities, to form a fire-fighting unit at Port Dinorwic and appointed six members 'who would be trained for this special duty in connection with air raids'. Another 34 members registered for the ARP classes held at the Church House, Port Dinorwic on Wednesday 25 October. [C&DH 27.10.39] Later a public meeting was held in the village to 'acquaint the public with the various means of notifying an Air Raid and what was required of the public'. [C&DH 1.11.39] If an air raid had occurred whilst children were attending school it was (naively) thought:

"...on the question of dispersal of children from schools in the event of an air raid...it would be better for the children to remain in the school under the control of the teacher rather than be allowed to run wild outside..."

As the number of air-raids increased during 1940, compulsory fire-watching was introduced and the Ministry of Labour directed men and women into Civil Defence and other services as an alternative to industrial employment. First Aid, Medical Services, Rescue and Demolition Services, Decontamination Service (in the event of a gas attack), Air Raid Wardens and Gas Detection Officers all formed part of the Civil Defence Services – the Air Raid Wardens being the best known as far as the general public was concerned. At first, all ages volunteered for Civil Defence but, as the young joined the armed forces, an appeal in June 1940 asked particularly for volunteers from among the over-50s.

The Minister of Home Security was also responsible for the safety of the public and, for those living in what were considered vulnerable areas of the country, they had the opportunity of having a shelter provided free of charge for those earning less that £250 a year. Over that figure you were expected to pay £7 towards the cost. In the first few weeks of the war over two million of these had been distributed to householders free of charge by local authorities

These structures, known as Anderson Shelters, were made of

corrugated steel sheeting of a size suitable to house an average size family during an air-raid and were considered to be safe and reasonably comfortable. The shelter was erected in a shallow hole dug in the garden with the sheets bolted together. It then had to be covered with earth to a depth of 15 inches on top and 30 inches on sides and back. This had to be done by 11 June 1940 otherwise 'substantial penalties' were liable to be inflicted. Others preferred to build a structure of brick and reinforced concrete roof 9 inches thick and this not only acted as a shelter but also a garden shed. Whatever type was used, many recalled having hot cocoa and a biscuit and listening to the sounds of planes overhead and wondering "Is it one of ours or one of theirs?". When possible, a shelter was lit by a single electric bare bulb or failing that one or two smelly paraffin lamps would provide a flickering light. [NLW Ms 23073D]

Other public shelters were built at various sites convenient for those away from home at the time of an air-raid and these would have specified above the doorway the maximum number of people that the shelter was capable of holding. As far as the people of Llandudno were concerned, a cave on the Great Orme, reputed to be able to accommodate 'thousands of people', had been prepared for use as a shelter had it been necessary. [GAS M/1566/111] 100,000 bricks were ordered by the Caernarvon Council from the local brickworks for 'Communal Air Raid Shelters' in various parts of the town. [C&DH 15.11.40]

Neighbours would quite often, if not staying in their own Anderson shelter, cellar or under the stairs, go to the same shelter thus forming an 'association' and under such circumstances there was a tendency for the usual British reserve to diminish as people chatted whether they knew each other or not.

On account of the role that the police (and Special Constables who were enrolled to assist) would play during the war the Home Office decided to issue 25,000 sandbags in March 1939 for the 'Protection of Police Buildings' but it was reported in the local newspaper that:

"...R T Jones (of Caernarvon) thought the provision was an unnecessary expense. Caernarvonshire he said had been classified as a receiving area and he could not imagine a stray aeroplane bombing village police stations like Llanberis ..." [C&DH 31.3.39]

At the time of the Munich crisis, air-raid precaution and anti-gas training classes had been conducted by the police at the Barracks in Caernarvon. [GAS XJ1234/10] The decision was taken that everyone would be issued with gas-masks especially after the experience of the First World War when poisonous gas had been used. Questions were being asked by the chairman of the Caernarvonshire County Council five months before war was declared as to when gas-masks were to be made available. A few had been received but they were only intended for practise purposes such as the Air Raid Precautions anti-gas training given at the Memorial Hall, Felinheli in June 1939. Caernarvon people received their allocation of gas-masks at the Pavilion over a period of three days from 8 September 1939. The face-mask was of simple construction covering the face completely and having retaining adjustable straps placed over the back of the head. Special contraptions with hand-pumps at the side to be operated by an adult were available to protect babies.

"If the gas rattles sound, put on your gas-masks at once wherever you are, even in bed" said the official leaflets. For a time, people obeyed, carrying them around in the standard cardboard containers in which they were issued. After a few months of war, however, there was a tendency for the 'little brown boxes' to be left at home.

Additional hospitals, such as the Gadlys Red Cross Auxiliary Hospital at Cemaes Bay, Anglesey were established to cater for possible military casualties which would be beyond the capacity of civilian hospitals. The property Gadlys was owned by three sisters, one being the matron, one the cook and the other responsible for general duties (PNP 187). An article in the *North Wales Chronicle*, which stated that patients were appreciative of the kindness shown by the staff, seemed at variance with a report written 15 May 1944 which suggested that all was not well at the hospital. Three ATS and eight WAAF patients were of the opinion:

"...Matron is continually snooping and intruding into their (patients) private pursuits; instead of the place proving a happy restful interlude between hospital treatment and the resumption of service duties it has become a very disagreeable place. Gadlys Hospital is apparently generally known by its patients and by service people outside as 'The Concentration Camp'..."

According to Lord Anglesey, Plas Newydd was being considered for use as a hospital:

"20.11.41. There is a great fight going on between Ministry of Health and Army Medical on the one hand and the War Department on the other because both want this (Plas Newydd) house; the one to make a hospital for the whole island which now has 70,000 inhabitants and 16 hospital beds and the other for accommodation for either Searchlight or Anti-Aircraft Batteries ..." (PNP 459-469)

Even as late as October 1944 part of Plas Newydd was offered by Lord Anglesey to the Joint War Committee of the British Red Cross and St John's Ambulance as a Convalescent Home. When the 29th British General Hospital, Royal Army Medical Corps (RAMC), arrived back from Egypt 11 December 1943, it established a base at Vaynol Park, near Bangor. The RAMC also had its 11th Casualty Clearing Station at the requisitioned *Bluebird Café* and *Waterloo Hotel* at Betws-y-Coed. Nearby Coed-y-Celyn was also requisitioned and utilised as a Red Cross Auxiliary Hospital and Rehabilitation Centre.

Although towns and villages of Gwynedd were subjected to aerial attacks the reporting of these events in local papers lacked details of the actual location because of the censorship applicable during the war. *

Royal Observer Corps

The Observer Corps had been formed before the start of the war for the purpose of reporting not only the movement of all aircraft, both friendly and enemy within a zone, but also of aircraft crashes and any changes in the weather pattern such as, "... the lowering of cloud base over hills, ground mist forming which would obscure the ground, electrical storms, heavy rainstorms, sea mists, snowstorms, sudden gales, strong winds...". In the days before the sophisticated flying instruments of today became available, weather conditions were of considerable importance to novice air-crew particularly when flying over mountainous terrain.

The Observation Posts were located in such a manner, usually some ten miles apart, that most parts of the country would be covered. They were manned by members of the corps, both men and women, full-time and part-time, who were trained to identify most types of aircraft and also to keep up to date with changes in design and style of camouflage. Training in identification was provided in various ways including model aircraft which they were supposed to identify blindfolded simply by touch! Members of the ROC were allowed to visit RAF airfields in the area to see several types of aircraft and to visit the Flying Control Rooms and the station

---

* some of the recorded incidents are listed in Appendix I.

Red Cross nursing staff at Coed-y-Celyn Auxiliary Hospital, Betws-y-Coed. The male figure top left is an Army Physical Training Instructor.
[Mrs Beti R Matthews]

Ambulance belonging to the 'War Organisation of the British Red Cross Society and Order of St John' at Coed-y-Celyn Auxiliary Hospital, Betws-y-Coed. Note the blackout covers on the headlamps.
[Mrs Beti R Matthews]

Wounded British servicemen, wearing hospital 'Blues' (with a red tie) at Coed-y-Celyn Auxiliary Hospital, Betws-y-Coed.
[Mrs Beti R Matthews]

Members of the Royal Observer Corps at Caernarfon Castle. When first formed, the ROC was not issued with uniforms and its members were identified by means of a striped arm band and a lapel badge. This photograph shows the Observers wearing their full uniform.
[Mrs Doris Rogers]

HRH Princess Marina, Duchess of Kent, inspecting members of the Royal Observer Corps, Caernarfon Castle.
[Mrs Doris Rogers]

Members of the Royal Observer Corps at Caernarfon Castle. Membership of the ROC was open to both men and women.
[Mr T Meirion Hughes]

cinemas where they were shown several 35mm training films. [UCNW BP31733]

Their observations, with detail of aircraft, height, direction of travel and speed, were relayed back to headquarters but their findings were not always regarded as good:

"The Height Finder methods of some posts are still very uncertain. Head Observers must see to it that their posts' crews are able to work their instruments efficiently and quickly. This is a most important part of an Observer's duties and is indispensable to Fighter Command..." [UCNW BGP 31695-742 Royal Observer Corps]

Members of the Observer Corps were on duty for a minimum of 24 hours per week, nevertheless, even at a time of war a memorandum had to remind those in charge of the question of National Insurance:

"... care should be taken when averaging over a week or two that these numbers do not exceed 27 hours more often than one in four otherwise they immediately fall within the insurable category. This does not alter the fact that all such members can be called upon to perform up to 48 hours a week when necessary ..." [UCNW BGP 31699/31701]

For a Leading Observer Class 'A' the scale of pay was £4.3.6 for a 48 hour week of which not less than 40 hours were spent on 'watch keeping duties' and the remainder on administration or instructional work. [UCNW BP 31705] When a certain standard in identification of planes had been achieved, members were rewarded with a certificate as was the case with O Pritchard of Post B2 Group 282 (headquarters at 31 Bangor Street, Caernarvon) who was able to identify not less than 25 out of 31 different aircraft and subsequently rewarded with a promotion in his rank.

Some reports on the observations made were not always complimentary:

"Air Raid Warnings – The Plotting and identification of aircraft by day has greatly improved though the one lone high aircraft in crowded areas still remains a problem. Plotting and identification by night is becoming more difficult. On October 24 (1941) a small force of enemy aircraft were engaged in mine laying between North Wales and the Isle of Man and occasionally came inland. One of these, Raid 145, crossed the track of a fighter in Caernarvon apparently J.28 square and the fighter was tracked hostile to Shrewsbury giving 9 yellow and 14 purple warnings. The enemy losing height, passed out to sea near Llandudno to lay mines, apparently not tracked. Controllers should always bear in mind the possibility of this happening and make every enquiry about the position of fighters not only from their own neighbouring RAF sector but also from other sectors ... In this particular case Atcham and Shrewsbury knew that a Beaufort was in this area at the time. Caernarvon did not. The ROC is not always informed where friendly fighters are operating". [UCNW Bangor Papers 31698]

On another occasion the Caernarvon section was complimented:

"... Valley sector have destroyed several enemy raiders in the last two weeks and a letter has been received thanking Caernarvon for their accurate plotting. In particular a report of flares at sea sent out by an enemy raider proved of real value and established the enemy's position. The enemy was intercepted and shot down ..."

Similar congratulatory messages were passed on in Anglesey on 1 September 1942:

"... Headquarters Royal Observer Corps 26 Bank Quay, Caernarvon. Recognition – Owing to the quick recognition of a Ju88 by A3 Post Rhosneigr the RAF were able to carry out an interception. Congratulations to this post and the Observers concerned. The Observers of this group as a whole are showing great keenness and are studying to keep themselves up to date as efficient Observers... [UCNW BP 31904]

"26.8.43 Post 2/A.1 Amlwch is to be congratulated on their vigilance and reporting of aircraft down in sea at night on August 21/22 all crew of five being saved." [UCNW BP 31707]

"28.8.44 Sea Rescues – I wish you to personally convey my congratulations and thanks to the member concerned with the reporting of raid A45-N dropping red flares and the tracking of dinghy out to sea in the early hours of Saturday morning 26 August 44. You will be pleased to know that seven airmen were rescued and brought safely to Llandwrog and are recovering in the sick bay at this airfield ... The aircraft was a Wellington ... Group Commandant, 28.2 Group ROC." [UCNW BP 31708]

The Observer Corps members were expected to report anything of a suspicious nature as they did on 21 October 1940:

"... whilst out on patrol suspicious winking or signalling lights were observed in an easterly direction from the square at Four Crosses. The attention of four members of the Home Guard who were on duty under Corporal D G Jones was drawn to the lights.

From observations made these lights seemed to be Morse signalling and came from the vicinity of Braich y Saint, Criccieth or its near vicinity... It is also known that the Observers then on duty at the Observers Post at Chwilog observed these lights ..." [GAS XM 806/2]

Initially the Observer Corps headquarters were installed in the Chamberlain Tower of Caernarvon Castle before taking over Eagle Tower with its canteen facilities. They worked an eight hour shift from 8am to 4pm followed by four hour shifts at night with two hours on and two hours off with beds provided for their rest period. A large plotting table was provided on which indicators would be placed to show the movement of both British and German planes, direction and height of flight. This information was relayed to them from Observers at posts in various parts of the surrounding area by telephone and received by them on their headphones with mouthpieces attached. Senior officers seated in an elevated position were then able to see the type of aircraft that were in their area and take the necessary action. Whenever German aircraft were observed the information was passed on to Ground Interception Control from where instructions were given for allied aircraft to deal with the enemy planes. All movements of the aircraft were also recorded on paper so that the complete course would be shown indicating where the plane had entered the zone and where exited.

Discipline was usually quite strict as shown in a letter dated 9 January 1942 from Capt. J W Sanders, HQ Caernarvon:

"... Welsh is still being used over operational lines at times causing confusion to brother posts ... This must cease forthwith ..."

On 1 May 1945 members were informed that the stand down of the Royal Observer Corps would begin simultaneously with the disbanding of the Civil Defence General Services on 4 May 1945 when all reporting would cease. Perhaps the final accolade for a Corps of men and women whose accurate and diligent observations had saved many lives was expressed in the final report:

"Future of the ROC: ... while it is not possible yet to foresee what changes the future may bring in the aircraft reporting system of this country, it is certain that at present there is no substitute for the skill and experience of Observers and it is still conceivable that a satisfactory substitute may not be found ..." [UCNW BP 31741]

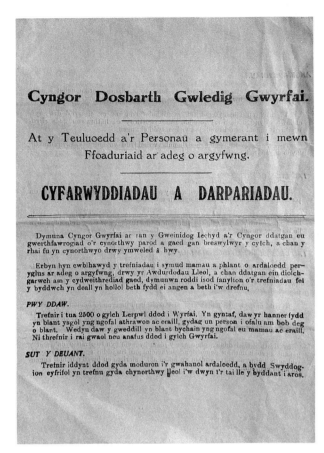

Posters in both English and Welsh were issued to request assistance with the billeting of Evacuees. [Mr Aled Jones]

CHAPTER 3: Evacuation

With the inevitability of war looming on the horizon, plans for the evacuation of children from the zones considered to be most at risk had been prepared well beforehand. Nevertheless, the task of moving approximately 3,000,000 schoolchildren from one place to another in a relatively short space of time, was formidable to say the least.

The Government Evacuation Scheme gave details of moving children below school age who were accompanied by their mothers, unaccompanied children of school age, expectant mothers and blind persons from 'evacuable' areas to 'evacuation' areas. Since the scheme was entirely voluntary, it was necessary for the Government to issue a Civil Defence leaflet in July 1939 to convince parents of the need to evacuate children and it was pointed out that:

> "It will not be possible to let you know in advance the place where your child will be going but you will be notified as soon as the movement is over...Of course it means heartache to be separated from your children, but you can be sure that they will be well looked after. They will relieve you of one anxiety at any rate..."

Many mothers with children under school age had to make an agonising decision as to whether to stay at home with their husbands and risk their very young children being maimed or even killed, or to leave for the comparative safety of the countryside. Others, instead of participating in the official evacuation scheme, preferred to make their own arrangements and stay with friends or relatives in the country, but they were warned that the government scheme would take priority and that there could be curtailment of both rail and road transport.

Of the Liverpool children who had been assembled at their individual schools on Sunday 3 September 1939, some were taken to Edge Hill Station and others to Lime Street Station where they boarded trains for various destinations. Most of the children were filled with foreboding for, as far as they were concerned, they were being separated from their parents for no apparent reason. Many were in tears; some had thoughts of a great adventure, believing that, at least for a little while, there would not be the usual confrontation with one or both parents for some misdemeanour or another.

The areas nearest to North Wales which were considered at risk were Liverpool, Bootle, Birkenhead and Wallasey. In some cases, the decision was taken to evacuate a whole school, both teachers and pupils, to a safer area for the duration of the emergency or until such time as it was felt that it was safe to return. A survey of all houses in Gwynedd in connection with the government evacuation scheme had been undertaken as early as February 1939 to establish where children could be accommodated. [C&DH 10.2.39] In anticipation of emergency accommodation being required initially in schools and village halls of Gwynedd, blankets and beds were brought by lorries from Liverpool and some families, rather than be separated from their children, fled the anticipated air attacks on Merseyside and brought their own furniture to rented houses in Caernarvon and the surrounding area.

A leaflet headed Cyngor Dosbarth Gwledig Gwyrfai and signed

by the Clerk to the Council and intended for advising the public, stated that of the initial 2,500 evacuees moved from Liverpool to Gwyrfai, half of them would be teachers and children and the other half smaller children with their mothers. It gave information on: how they would travel, what they would bring with them and various other points such as billeting allowance, how to deal with illness, complaints, schooling and entertainment.

The first communication between Liverpool Education Authority and its equivalent in Anglesey was received on 13 July 1939 and outlined the arrangements that would be put in hand in the event of a National Emergency. The original plan had been for 675 children to arrive from Alsop High School, Oulton High School and the Blue Coat School but eventually 2,468 arrived in the first contingent. For the first week or two, several schools were closed to Anglesey children so that the Liverpool children and their teachers might have a place to assemble. Anglesey teachers were available to help resolve difficulties and to assist their Liverpool colleagues with the large numbers of problems that arose.

The arrival of 2,000 children and teachers at Bangor coincided with the announcement being made by the Prime Minister, Neville Chamberlain – and relayed by Tannoy system in Deiniol Road– that war had been declared with Germany. From the railway station the children walked to the Central School where they were given a meal before being medically examined. Suspected cases of scabies, diphtheria or scarlet fever were taken to the County or Borough Hospitals for further examination and possible treatment. [C&DH 15.3.39]

The first contingent of Liverpool evacuees for Caernarvon arrived at the town station at 4.30pm on 1 September from where they were marched to the County School. There they were medically examined, and were given tea and a bag of rations which had to last them for the next 48 hours. It was 10.30pm before the exhausted children were eventually billeted for the night.

More children from the Cling Road, Heyworth Street and Earle Council Schools arrived during the next couple of days and were taken to Bontnewydd Orphanage; youth hostels at Glyn Padarn, Snowdon Ranger and Bryn Dinas (in Nantgwynant); the Royal Victoria Hotel, Llanberis; the CS Holiday Home at Betws Garmon and other locations. An opinion was expressed in a local paper that chapel school rooms, many of which had cooking facilities, should be converted into dormitories and that use might be made of the Caernarvon Pavilion which could be converted into suitable school premises.

Many of the evacuees were found to be in a very impoverished state with little if any change of clothing and some householders with whom they had been billeted, took the trouble, at their own expense, to reclothe them and supply new footwear only to find that many of these children returned home a few weeks later. [C&DH 29.9.39]

If the actual arrangements of transferring children from Liverpool to various towns had been well organised, information about their life-style and living conditions was sadly lacking. For many of the evacuees a bath night (taken in a tin bath in front of the fire) was a new experience. Many children from the poorer areas of the large towns and cities arrived infested with lice and had to be quickly treated before other children were inflicted with the same problem.

"There is certainly one thing that reception areas have a right to protest against and that is sending dirty and verminous children and people into their areas" [C&DH 8.9.39]

The staple diet of fish and chips which many of the evacuees were used to caused many problems for the hosts when attempts were made to find acceptable alternative fare. Some of the children who came to North Wales were adept at stealing and shop-lifting as a way of life and therefore resented the inevitable chastisement and correction which followed. Even with such obvious potential problems, any householder who refused to comply with the requirements of a billeting order was liable to be taken to court and fined up to £25.

Weekly billeting allowances relating to evacuated children were: under five years of age 8/6d; 5-10 years of age 10/6d; 10-12 11/-; 12-14 12/-; 14-16 13/-; 16 15/6d; 17 and over 16/6d. The allowance for a teacher was 5/- per week for accommodation only; any food supplied was by arrangement between teacher and householder. A similar arrangement applied with a mother and child under school age with accommodation being charged at 5/- for the mother and 3/- for the child.

In some cases, free mid-day meals, halibut liver oil capsules and iron tablets were also provided. If they had to be paid for, then the cost was 2d per week for the capsules and 1d for the tablets. Just before Christmas the City of Liverpool increased the evacuation allowance by 2/- per child to cover extras over the festivities. The Liverpool authorities were also asked to send sufficient numbers of school nurses and dentists who were to remain in the county for the duration of the war in order to attend to evacuated children. [C&DH 1.12.39]

Organisations such as the Women's Voluntary Service (WVS) assisted with the influx of the evacuees and did much by starting clothing depots so as to reclothe those children who came from deprived areas. Since clothing and footwear were strictly rationed, it was necessary to issue supplementary coupons to allow them to have a change of clothing. When boots required repairing, assuming that leather was available, it invariably meant that evacuated children had either to stay indoors until their footwear was returned or walk about bare footed. Some assistance was also received from Liverpool with additional clothing being sent for the children.

The provision of education for both local and evacuated children was as much a problem on Anglesey as it was on the mainland. The initial reaction of the local education authority was to dismiss the idea of educating both sets of children in the same premises because of language problems, children only receiving part-time education and problems for teachers in preserving the identity of their schools:

"...education of the English children has to be in their own language if it is to be effective but the teaching of Anglesey children must not be impaired since the important function of our schools at this time is to safeguard the language, culture and traditions of Wales ..."
[UCNW BP 4594]

Owing to the number of children evacuated to the village of Port Dinorwic, and the constraints of space within the Council and National schools, it was decided that until alternative accommodation was available, schooling would have to be on a two shift system. During the first week the local children were taught until 12.45pm and the Earle Road Senior Girls, of which there were 150, would then attend under Miss A Haslam, headmistress from 1.15pm to 5pm. The following week the visitors attended in the morning and the locals in the afternoon. By October 1939 the times of attendance had been changed to 9 - 12pm and 1 - 4pm. Eventually, the evacuated children received their lessons at the Memorial Hall.

Even though every effort was made to help the children to settle in to their new environment and to entertain them by showing educational films as well as the old favourites such as Laurel and Hardy, by November 1939, 141 children had returned home to Liverpool from Port Dinorwic alone.

Initially, children from Liverpool were inclined to stay together because they were taught in their own classes by their own teachers and would only mix to a certain extent with local children. For many of the children, this was their first experience of seeing the countryside and being able to participate in nature walks, and those who were billeted on farms or small holdings enjoyed sharing in the daily routine.

The children destined for Beddgelert were taken to a school where they were allocated to local families. One girl, Eileen Hunt, who stayed with Hugh O. Williams, a headmaster, and his wife and seventeen year old daughter, recalls hearing through an open window the sound of an evacuee crying on their first night in the village. To reassure Eileen's parents, the headmaster wrote them a letter:

"As you probably know we are a little village at the foot of Snowdon and one of the beauty spots of North Wales. Our climate all round the year is pleasant but a bit wet. About 70 children arrived here from the same school as your little girl and I happened to be in charge of finding billets for them. As two were to stay with me I, during the sorting out at our local school, looked about for "two nice little girls" – those were my instructions from my wife... I really must say here that you have a charming child nicely brought up. She is lovely in the house – very polite and has settled down well. Naturally she talks of Daddy and Mammy and at times is a little homesick especially after a visit from her mother but I have a daughter of 17 and a maid of similar age and they are both fond of children and together with my wife they soon have her happy again. My wife says she will be sorry when she has to part with her and we all shall be pleased to take care of her till this war is over and then hand over to you a happy child. She asked me quietly this morning if I could find a house for her mother somewhere near and I hope towards the end of the week to fulfil her wish and my promise to your wife and hope to find billet for her in a modern bungalow with kind people about a mile from here and then she will be able to see her girlie very often. There is certainly no need to pay me anything for what you are good enough to call kindness nor for anything we may give Eileen - She deserves it all as one who served in the last war and a lover of children can assure you that we shall take every care of your dear little girl ..."

For another couple in Port Dinorwic, Eileen Oldfield, a little girl of seven years of age who came to stay with them from Liverpool, was a timely replacement, albeit temporarily, for their only daughter whom they had recently lost through illness. The evenings were occupied by playing games of ludo, snakes and ladders and draughts as well as reading stories. Within twelve months Eileen was sufficiently accomplished in Welsh to be able to participate in both chapel services and the eisteddfod.

Where brothers and sisters had been evacuated together they naturally clung to each other in a strange environment and would resent any attempt to separate them when it came to finding a place for them to stay. Three young evacuee sisters, Sarah, Dorothy and Hilda Woodward, after surviving a seemingly endless journey, and resisting all attempts to billet them in separate houses, eventually found themselves in the quarry village of Llanberis. They knew that they had arrived in a strange land because they could not understand a word of what the people were saying nor, quite often, could they make themselves understood. They saw many strange words which they did not understand like *Bechgyn* (Boys) and *Genethod* (Girls) above the doors leading into the local school.

Because the billeting allowance was only paid until a child was fourteen years of age, most of those over that age returned to Liverpool. In the case of the three sisters, when the two elder ones had departed leaving the youngest on her own, she found herself becoming integrated naturally into village life and the 'foreign' language was soon learnt without the necessity of enforced schooling. Consequently, this opened a new world to the young visitor who was able to converse in the Welsh language to the extent that she, like Eileen Oldfield, was able to compete at local eisteddfodau and participate in religious services.

The degree of welcome varied enormously from billet to billet and no doubt this would reflect greatly on the happiness of the child and how soon he or she settled in the new environment. In some cases, the degree of integration resulted in some children, who had spent their formative years away from their natural parents, refusing to return home at the end of the war. Even when persuasion was successful, the return was made with reluctance and it took some a good twelve months before they settled down.

Many of the evacuated children were virtually adopted by Welsh families for the duration of their stay and benefited physically and spiritually from their experience, in some cases so much so that they never returned home or if they did, they returned time and time again to 'Uncles' and 'Aunts' from whom they had received so much kindness and happiness. In the days of rationing and shortages, the kindly people who welcomed them into their homes must have sacrificed a great deal to make them comfortable and happy for the duration of their stay. Unfortunately, not all the evacuated children had fond memories of their stay in North Wales and were relieved to return home.

It was not only the Merseyside local authority schools that were evacuated to north west Wales; many urban 'private' schools also decided to move to the relative security of the countryside for the duration of hostilities. HMS *Conway,* a cadet school ship, catering for boys aged between $13^{1/2}$ and $16^{1/2}$, had been located at Rock Ferry on Merseyside since the late 19th century. Boys who successfully completed the two years' course were accepted by the Ministry of Transport as having one year's sea service towards qualifying for the 2nd Mate Certificate of Competency Examination. Owing to the danger of possible air attacks early in the war, the vessel of 4,375 tons (which had started life as HMS *Nile* in 1839) was towed to a new anchorage in the Menai Strait and moored off Bangor in 1941. In this instance, the move proved to be permanent and in 1949 the school ship was relocated off Plas Newydd, Anglesey.

With the possibility of war being declared John Leakey the headmaster of Dulwich College in South London drew up plans for the evacuation of pupils from the school to Coursehorn near Cranbrook in Kent but, as the result of the Dunkirk evacuation and the subsequent vulnerability of the south coast to possible German invasion and bombing, enquiries started to be made for alternative accommodation.

Word was received of the possibility of finding accommodation in Betws-y-Coed and a member of the staff visited the *Waterloo Hotel* only to find that the Royal Army Medical Corps had taken it over as a military hospital. However, all was not lost because a little further down the road they found the seventeenth century *Royal Oak Hotel* and, once the normal guests had vacated their rooms, the school took up residence.

The overcrowding which the pupils experienced at the hotel was soon alleviated when the proprietor of the *Llugwy Tea Rooms* and accompanying boarding house, offered his property to the school, an offer which was gladly accepted. Thirty-eight boys from the Junior Department were housed upstairs while the tea rooms were used as form rooms and a dining room. Other rooms for teaching and for use as a gymnasium were found in the converted coaching stables on the other side of the road to the hotel.

Until the parents received a circular from Betws-y-Coed a few days after the arrival of the boys, they had no idea where their

Pupils of Dulwich College receiving physical training instruction on the lawn of the Royal Oak Hotel, Betws-y-Coed. [Dulwich College]

HMS Conway, *the naval training school was housed in the former warship HMS* Nile. *This photograph shows the ship aground near the Menai Suspension Bridge in 1953. [Seiont II Maritime Trust]*

children had been taken. Nevertheless the situation was generally accepted by parents and only two boys were withdrawn from the school. As far as the expense of moving the pupils was concerned, the government was not prepared to pay the £700 required to cover the cost of transport and alterations to the hotel, but the parents generously contributed £800.

For the five years that the school was at Betws, the average working time for the headmaster, his wife and the staff was in excess of twelve hours a day. Even during the holidays some of the boys remained at the school which entailed some of the staff being on duty. But, as John Leakey states in his book *School Errant*:

> "...(it) does not show a true picture of the unending and devoted labour which the staff gave so freely during the five years, nor of the heavy responsibility for so many children's lives in which they took their full share..."

The boys became fully integrated within the local community and participated in various schemes such as collecting salvage, helping with the National Savings campaign, the making of camouflage nets for the army in the *Royal Oak* stables and carrying out work in conjunction with the Forestry Commission. As the result of this latter enterprise, part of a nearby plantation was named after the school.

Whilst in the forests collecting wood for the fires, the boys took the opportunity to collect sphagnum moss which grew in profusion and which was used in its dried form to supplement cotton-wool for wound dressings. Male fern, foxgloves and nettles, which were used for medicaments and dye, were also collected for Bangor University and, in the autumn, rose hips.

There were at least three other schools evacuated to the Betws-y-Coed area, namely Edenthorpe School which was resident at the *Coed Derw Hotel* in 1940 with Miss Bullock as headmistress, Kent House School at Plas Maenan and Aubyns Private School for Boys in Voelas Hall. Once Dulwich College had been established at the *Royal Oak Hotel*, Mrs Barnett, the wife of a master, started a school class for a few girls of around nine years of age in a small café nearby.

To commemorate their stay in Betws-y-Coed, an appeal launched in 1979 by Dulwich School was associated with the Snowdonia National Park Visitors Centre which opened in 1985 in the restored *Royal Oak Hotel* stables which had served as classrooms for the school during the war.

Directly after the Dunkirk evacuation, the Lake House School in Bexhill, Sussex was requisitioned by the army and it became necessary for the pupils and staff to be evacuated in June 1940. They arrived at the *Royal Victoria Hotel*, Llanberis, which they were to share with the army. The headmaster, Mr Alan Hugh Williams, together with three assistant masters and 40 pupils stayed there until September 1940 when they moved to the requisitioned *Penygwryd Hotel* (Arthur Lockwood, the licensee had to move out of the hotel and into the nearby house for the duration of their stay) four miles from Capel Curig. By 1943, the number of pupils had declined and the decision was taken to leave North Wales for a small village near Kirby Lonsdale.

CHAPTER 4: Home Guard and Police Force

When the Local Defence Volunteers (LDV) (later to be renamed the Home Guard) were established on 14 May 1940, Sir Anthony Eden, the Secretary of State for War, appealed for volunteers aged between 17 and 65 to help the regular forces at a time when there was a strong possibility of invasion following the German successes in France and the Low Countries.

The LDV (which to some unkind individuals meant 'Look, Duck and Vanish') were trained by those who had seen service in the First World War or by Regular army personnel and by the time they had been moulded into something like a defensive unit, the original LDV armband had been abandoned for a full uniform and US rifles of First World War vintage had been issued instead of the initial pitchforks and broom handles. Members of the Caernarvonshire LDV were allowed to use the rifle range at Glynllifon but, as the letter dated 9.7.40 from Brigade Major HQ 23rd Army Tank Regiment, Glynllifon Park showed, all was not well:

> "... your LDVs turned up and shot on our range yesterday. They were very keen and showed considerable confidence in their rifles. Unfortunately a very high proportion of the ammunition was dud and they were only able to fire four out of their ten shots ..." [GAS 1301/19]

The initial task for the Local Defence Volunteers, was to produce some semblance of a defence force and instructions were issued:

> "...MOBILE ARMED PARTY – this party needs constant training in rifle shooting and the handling of arms so as to form it into a workmanlike and efficient unit capable of rapid and precise movement..."

> "...ROAD BLOCKING Duties of LDV – 23 June 1940 - A census should be taken of all the available road blocking material in the neighbourhood of the proposed block – this means questioning at the farms around in order to find what carts, ploughs, harrows etc. are available..." [GAS XM/1301/6, 11]

Within three months, the initial 250,000 volunteers had grown to a million and at the same time the title was changed to Home Guard. Eventually, all men who were not eligible for the forces or specified services and aged between 17 and 65 had to join. Members of the Home Guard were expected to present themselves for training for 48 hours each month and were liable to be prosecuted if this figure was not attained.

In the Caernarvonshire sector, it was at 'nodal points' (i.e. intersection of roads) such as those at Beddgelert, Penygwryd, Betws-y-Coed and Llanrwst that the Home Guard:

> "...must be prepared to resist all forms of attack. Resistance at these places must be maintained to the last man and the last round. In order to make plans to stock these places with ammunition, food, water and medical stores, it is necessary to know how many men will carry out the defence at each place...please consider each nodal point and say what strength of garrison you recommend should be brought into each place...
> Major Dolman, Craig y Dderwen, Betws y Coed 24.7.42..."

Other places considered suitable were Aberglaslyn, where 20 men would be responsible for four road blocks, on the Beddgelert to Penygwryd road where there was one road block a short way out of the village with 16 men, and similarly on the Beddgelert to Caernarvon road where there would be one road block on the edge of the village. [GAS XM/1301/6] It was the task of the Local Defence Volunteers to inspect bridges to ensure that no preparation had been made for demolition by saboteurs. The Capel Curig contingent was commanded by Major Arthur Lockwood from Penygwryd (he had been the licensee of the hotel since about 1906 when he had come to the area to build the power station at Cwm Dyli).

When large scale exercises were due to take place in March 1942, owing to the lack of private telephones and radios, the officer commanding asked the postmaster at Caernarvon if his troops could make free calls because "it is difficult to ensure that each man engaged in such exercise has a sufficient supply of coppers on him".

Officers and men of the Penygroes Home Guard outside the village school. Those wearing medal ribbons are probably ex-servicemen from the First World War. [Mr Aled Jones]

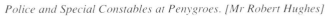

Police and Special Constables at Penygroes. [Mr Robert Hughes]

The request was refused and an urgent appeal was issued asking for those with motor cycles to perform the duty of Despatch Riders for the Home Guard one night a week. They would be issued with full uniform (waterproof clothing was not provided) with the white Royal Corps of Signals armlet, boots, steel helmet and equipment but crash helmets, normally worn by Despatch Riders, were not yet available. An allowance of 2d a mile to cover the cost of petrol, licence, insurance and running repairs was paid to the owners of the machines which were being operated on Home Guard duties. Petrol coupons were available for such a duty and an allowance given for wear and tear. Apparently when the first appeal for motor cyclists was answered it was mainly by 1914-18 veterans but other attempts were made to entice the younger element to enlist.

As an additional method of communication the National Pigeon Service was available and the local representatives were R A Bridges, North Road, Caernarvon, R Williams, Cartref, Ala Road, Pwllheli and Robert Evans, 3 Clifton Road, Llandudno. But in the event of an invasion the following instructions were issued:

> "...Destruction of pigeons in invasion – In any area which is likely to fall into the hands of the enemy all homing pigeons other than those in use for Army, Royal Air Force or other official purposes will be destroyed to prevent their use by the enemy. It will also be necessary as far as practical to destroy or dismantle lofts used by such pigeons in order to prevent any pigeons which may be flying out at the time of destruction from returning to the loft later..." [GAS XJ1234/42]

Civil Defence leaflet advising people of what steps to take in the event of invasion by the Germans. The quality of translation would not be tolerated today.
[MrAled Jones]

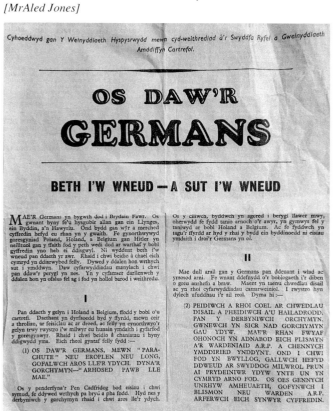

Members of the Home Guard were expected to assist the police in their duties:

> "...Object – to check the movement of enemy agents while not slowing up the movement of troops or essential services... examination shall be carried out by police...there will be a detachment of Home Guard or regular troops in concealed positions from which they can cover the block by fire..."

The method of 'Halting Motorists' was given:

> "...By day – the sentry should use the ordinary police signals.
> By night – the sentry should stop motor traffic by waving a red lamp. In either case there should be another man 20 yards behind the sentry stopping traffic who is ready to fire if the car refuses to stop..."

The inconvenience caused to the public by the government directive to obliterate place names on road signs, railway and underground stations, post offices and telephone boxes was considered insignificant as compared to the problems confronting possible invaders requiring directions.

A directive dated 16.9.40 from General Staff, Kinmel Sub Area, Llanerch Park, St Asaph stated:

> "It is likely that at the time of invasion Germans will be landed in British battle dress mainly by air but possibly also by sea...All HQ units will therefore ensure that methods of identification are at all times strictly enforced..." [GAS XM.1301/11]

Consequently, checking identification passes at road blocks presented the Home Guard with problems because of the many Allied forces of different nationalities, vagrants and people of no fixed abode passing through the county. A list showing 16 different types of Identity Cards in use by various people merely added to the confusion.

The Royal Welch Fusiliers Regimental Depot at Wrexham, which had become the Infantry Training Centre at the start of the war, was also on stand-by in case of invasion and was expected to take certain action on receiving the code word 'Cromwell' which was to indicate that the invasion was imminent or had started. The depot received a message over the telephone which was scribbled on a piece of paper and left in a tray to await action. When it was eventually found and acted upon, soldiers were ordered to their appointed stations. At Rhiw, on the Lleyn peninsula, a small contingent arrived followed by their commanding officer driving his 1935 Hillman Minx car carrying his twelve-bore shotgun – in case he had time to spare for a shoot. After languishing there for three weeks, during which time a number of game birds were disposed of, the Company Commander based at the *Oakley Arms*, Tanybwlch bade them return to headquarters to await further instructions.

Although church bells were to be used as a warning when an invasion was taking place, it had been decided that church towers could only be used for observation and communication but not for military purposes 'no offensive weapons or searchlight to be installed and incumbent to remain in charge of the church and tower'. [GAS XM 1301/9]

In the summer of 1940, every household in Gwynedd was given a Government leaflet printed in English and Welsh and entitled: "If the Invader Comes - What to do – and how to do it." :

> "...The Germans threaten to invade Great Britain. If they do they will be driven out by our Navy, our Army and our Air Force. Yet the ordinary men and women of the civilian population will also have their part to play. Hitler's invasion of Poland, Holland and Belgium was greatly helped by the fact that the civilian population was taken by surprise. They did not know what to do when the moment came. You must not be taken by surprise..."

"...Remember that if parachutists come down near your home, they will not be feeling at all brave. They will not know where they are, they will have no food, they will not know where their companions are. They will want you to give them food, means of transport and maps. They will want you to tell them where they have landed, where their comrades are, and where our own soldiers are..."

Problems arising with over-enthusiastic members of the Home Guard who regarded every parachutist as the invading German army and shot at everything in sight, necessitated the issuing of the following instructions:

"...Cases have occurred recently of our own pilots descending by parachute being injured by our own forces. All ranks of the Army and all members of Home Guard must clearly understand the following instructions:

1. If fewer than six parachutists are seen descending they will not be fired at.

2. When parachutists are airmen in distress, either British or German, their aircraft will probably be seen or heard to crash in the neighbourhood at the same time.

3. The Air Ministry has issued the following instructions to RAF personnel forced to land by parachute.

a. When persons approach to apprehend them they should stand still holding both hands over their heads with fingers extended and announce their identity loudly. They should make no movement until their identity is established.

b. If ordered to produce proof of identity they should say where this can be found on them but should not lower their hands in case this action arouses suspicion that they are reaching for a weapon.

c. If injured they should lie flat and stay still.

(courtesy of Clwyd County Council – *The Home Front: World War II*)

However, on other occasions it was stated that German airforce personnel who had landed in this country either by parachute or by crashed aircraft had been able to remain at large, some times, for hours and 'sometimes they have voluntarily surrendered to totally indifferent bystanders'. [GAS XM 1301/2]

Llanberis 'C' Company, Home Guard organised a full training programme during the winter of 1941-42 which included small arms, rifle and machine guns, grenades and bayonet, map reading, signalling, camouflage, tank hunting and destruction, fieldcraft, tactical exercises, guerrilla warfare, discipline and morale. [GAS XM/1301/13] Even though they had been supplied with flame-throwers, their use was restricted to the quantity of petrol available and 'it would be necessary for them to apply for coupons like everyone else'!

Whenever training took place at Belan Fort camp, rules were issued stating that the cookhouse and the aerodrome were out of bounds to all ranks except those employed therein. It was also necessary to warn all ranks 'of the danger of throwing stones etc. into the minefield (which was clearly marked) or interfering with them (the mines) in any way'. It seemed ominous for the following to be added:

"...Training: It is also the Medical Officer's wish that there should be a few men in each section who have an elementary knowledge of First Aid. The quick removal of the killed and immediate attention to the wounded will do much to keep up the morale of the fighting men..."

Whether such recommendation was made because of the following observation is not recorded:

"...Standard of training in Anglesey is not high enough: some Home Guard members cannot hit a 4 ft target at 200 yards..."

Exercise 'Dwrog' was intended to check the Llandwrog airfield and Belan Fort defences and a detachment from the Royal Welch Fusiliers, the 560th Coast Regiment RA and 3rd Caernarvonshire Bn Home Guard took part. It was intended that 'A' Company 3rd Caerns. HG was to proceed by boat at 07.30 (provided that the

HOME GUARD,
3rd (Caernarvonshire Bn.,
"A" Company.

No. 2 Platoon.
December 3, 1940.

Section Leaders,
Sub-Section Leaders,
Volunteers.

Your earnest attention is drawn to this memorandum.

Weather permitting, Saturday afternoon and Sunday open-air training will continue, but the importance of attending Musketry, Lewis Gun, Signalling Classes, etc., during the winter evenings cannot be over-emphasised.

Volunteers in the Home Guard have undertaken an honourable obligation, not only to do a job of work, but also to train and drill to do that work efficiently. Regular and punctual attendance in classes is therefore imperative. The few Volunteers who have drawn clothing and equipment, and who are absenting themselves consistently from classes and parades do not fulfil their promises, and they are jeopardising the ultimate efficiency of the unit.

Efficiency follows discipline. An enthusiastic Home Guardsman welcomes discipline, and obeys orders unreservedly. He becomes a friend of his Superior Officer, Section Leader and Sub-Section Leader after the "dismiss."

Non-attendance or lateness on parade lead to slackness. Familiarity with Officers and N.C.O.'s will end in slackness and inefficiency.

Standing about, waiting for volunteers, who are late for class or parade, is waste of good time. This is not the time to be idle. Serious and important work is to be done, and it must be tackled wholeheartedly.

Road defences, etc., will not be of much use unless the Volunteers manning them are properly trained and inculcated with "team spirit" to win.

Training takes time, but Home Guardsmen must submit to intensive training, which means hard but interesting work.

A public parade, well done, is good drill. Steadiness in the ranks is imperative, but the admiration of the crowd must wait until the work solemnly pledged to achieve is done.

The slogan now is ACTUAL TRAINING.

*Instruction leaflet issued to 'A' Company,
3rd (Caernarvonshire) Bn., Home Guard.
[Mrs Margaret Sheldon]*

weather was suitable) from Caernarvon to Belan Fort with its three light machine guns and two naval guns and held by 403rd Coast Battery RA. After successfully negotiating the mines laid on the beach, they were then confronted by a furious Commanding Officer yelling in a rage, "Get off my bloody runways!" when he thought his flying schedules were going to be interrupted by these interlopers.

As late as 1942, in a document described as Consolidated Instructions to Invasion Committees in England and Wales it stated:

"...The general military plan for our troops is that there will be no withdrawal and that such enemy forces as penetrate will be counter-attacked and destroyed or driven into the sea..." 6th Marquess of Anglesey, Lt. Col. OC No. 3 Battalion Home Guard Anglesey. [PNP 459]

At the same time, women were asked to form committees:

"...and all are invited to come and learn how to be of the greatest use in the case of invasion. The Women's Home Defence do not drill or wear uniform but they do learn Self-Defence, Anti-Gas Treatment, First-Aid, Field Cooking etc. Do not forget that the Germans have proved themselves to be ruthless barbarians, sparing neither women nor children but using them in the most brutal fashion and killing them without mercy..." [PNP474]

Most of the local factories had their own Home Guard contingent formed from their own employees. NECACO's detachment, with Major Jackson in charge and housed at The Lodge, was responsible for security at Llanberis; Peblig, Central Garage, Victory Works at Caernarvon and also the store section at Schofield's yard by Pont Seiont, Caernarvon. However, the officer commanding No. 3 Platoon was rather critical of an exercise called 'Padarn' which took place in February 1942:

> "...he (Jackson) relied too much on 'token strength'. On paper he has 60 men to call upon from Llanberis but in actual fact less that 20 turned out. Can these others be relied upon in actual emergency? Speaking from my own experience in the Home Guard I much doubt it and I think it would be better for such men to receive the 'order of the boot' forthwith; obviously the number of men at Major Jackson's disposal were very inadequate for the job in hand. A point in favour of conscription..."

All the employees at the factories received periodic instructions that they were not to talk about their work to anyone. The ubiquitous "Careless Talk Costs Lives" poster to be seen in the factories, was a further reminder, if such was required, about their responsibility. L C Hunting, Chairman at NECACO issued on 1 December 1940 what was described as an Important Notice:

> "All works Personnel are hereby notified that Machine Guns have been posted throughout the area covering the works on both sides of the lake. These posts are manned day and night. Armed patrols are working in the vicinity also day and night in addition to the guards at the usual fixed points...necessary for all personnel to stop at once if challenged..." [GAS Q1783]

The Saunders Roe factory at Beaumaris also had its Home Guard detachment but because some of the members lived in Bangor they were told that if the Menai Bridge were destroyed they were to muster on Bangor pier where they would be picked up by launch. They had plenty of armaments to defend the factory including 57 rifles, 5 Light Machine Guns, 1 Light Browning Automatic Rifle, 1 Heavy Browning Machine Gun, 14 Sten Guns together with various grenades. However, the welfare of the men was very much in mind when they appointed Private Gravenell to be in charge of the catering and he and six ladies were to take over the canteen in an emergency.

The Daimler factory in Bangor also was guarded by its own Home Guard volunteers but the responsibility of looking after the Port Penrhyn stores was delegated to the storekeepers. These three stalwarts had the advantage of sitting in the comfort of the office and gazing through the window in the direction of Beaumaris and beyond thus ensuring that nothing untoward was happening within their line of vision. Provided the weather was fine and the forecast reasonable, two out of the three would take a walk along the quay while the third member took turns in preparing refreshments and manning the telephone. At night, when nothing could be seen through the window, they took on the role of Fire Watching which gave them an opportunity of improving their card playing.

They were never provided with a uniform, not even an arm band to signify their role, possibly because they were not entirely sure whether they were members of the Home Guard or Air Raid Wardens. The only form of protection which they had was a piece of wood but no instructions had been given as to its use if the occasion arose. There had been a rumour that a twelve-bore gun was kept in a locked cupboard but they never found the key to establish whether or not it was true.

In order that morale in the Home Guard be maintained a competition was arranged between sections within the Battalion on 6 November 1942 to 'foster a competitive spirit within the sector'. It was intended that points would be awarded and prizes given to the winners based on:

> "...Battle Drill; Battle Craft including turnout, smartness of movement, words of command. NB Turn out will be as 'for a Fighting Soldier NOT as for Ceremonial Parade..."

On 15 August 1942 the Pentraeth Home Guard organised an Open Athletic Sports day at Bryniau Field with competitions for children, Open, Platoon and Home Guard events only. Admission was 6d and the proceeds were in aid of British Red Cross and Prisoners of War Fund. Another public relations event was arranged for the Liverpool Blue Coat Hospital school at Beaumaris and a letter of appreciation dated 15 October 1942 was received by Major Arnold from John Bingham, Liverpool Blue Coat Hospital, Liverpool.

There were occasions when certain appointments proved unpopular with the men as was shown in a letter of 3 October 1940 addressed to a Dr. Parry and stating:

> "...we the undersigned...beg to draw your attention to the discord which is displayed in our platoon following a recent appointment made by Mr E Thomas our Company Commander. We would be glad if you could meet us so that we can discuss the matter with you. We have no objection whatsoever to Mr E Thomas being present at this meeting and we would like to point out that this communication is prompted only by a very sincere need for harmony in our platoon..."

The letter was signed by 31 members of the Llanberis platoon of the 3rd Bn Caernarvonshire Home Guard. [GAS XM1301/13]

Members of the Home Guard were liable to be prosecuted for absenteeism and in a leaflet issued by R J Wordsworth, Colonel Commanding the Snowdon Section, on 17 August 1943 it stated:

> "...Checking absenteeism is most distasteful to Home Guard officers...as in some cases the delinquent may be a friend, neighbour or sometimes a client of the Home Guard Officer concerned..."

When the Junior Officers of the 1st Bn Anglesey Home Guard celebrated their Second Annual Dinner at *The Bull Hotel*, Llangefni, Wednesday 24 February 1943 the 'Austerity Menu' stated:

> "...There'll be some soup, I've been promised a bit of pork and/or beef, we can get vegetables alright, we'll put on a good sweet..." [PNP 470]

This was in marked contrast to the fare which the Felinheli (Port Dinorwic) Home Guard contingent experienced. They met at a house called Menai View on Brynffynnon Road but the cookhouse was conveniently situated on the other side of the road in the National school where the meal, such as it was, was eaten while sitting at a child's desk. It was there that the culinary prowess of two retired sea captains was put to the test, for they were the official cooks for the local detachment numbering some thirty men. Normally, their expertise only stretched to boiling a kettle for a cup of tea but, they did manage occasionally to produce a dish of *lobscaws* (Irish stew), which, after a hard day's work, if not a gastronomic experience, was at least palatable. When it came to menu identification it was carried out in a simplistic way: if it had salt in it, it was a stew; if it had sugar in it, it was a pudding. [NLW 23037 D]

At Port Dinorwic, everyone had to be on parade by 6pm and remain at their post until 6am when breakfast of purported porridge was produced by the intrepid maritime experimenters and eaten prior to returning to work on a very heavy stomach. Since it would be expecting too much of the men to drill under such adverse conditions, this was usually undertaken in an evening or at the weekends in the vicinity of their 'headquarters'.

Accommodation was always a problem since every available building had been requisitioned for some purpose or another. In the case of the Home Guard at Rhostryfan, the old waiting room of the

Welsh Highland Railway was utilised as accommodation after repairs had been carried out. The Rhyd Ddu section also used a waiting room and booking office of the same railway. Carmel, Cesarea and Nebo Council Schools were used two or three nights a week where 'efficient black-out' had been fitted even though paraffin lamps were the only form of lighting. When the Caernarvon LDV force was first formed they used the North East tower of the Castle as did the ARP wardens. [GAS XM1301/20] Although the Caernarvon Home Guard had been offered the town's Institute Building for training it was not considered suitable and, unfortunately, the Drill Hall, which was their first choice, had been taken over by the Ministry of Labour. Because of such intransigence on the part of the staff, there had been a strong possibility of the Home Guard taking over the building by force but before that became necessary the Ministry of Labour left to take up residence in Siloh chapel schoolroom.

Unfortunately, when exercises were held on a Saturday or Sunday, this would be the time when school children were usually at a loose end and looking for trouble. They had the disconcerting ability of finding the men, although heavily camouflaged, and following the units through fields and woods. This would be one such occasion when the men realised that their leaders were not up to the task when they could not even deal with these unwelcome spectators. A report made in August 1941 described the 'Arfon' exercise as a farce because a machine-gun was surrounded by a crowd of children 'and the position of other hidden posts being given away to the enemy by the attitude of onlookers'.

Many police stations in North Wales, even as late as 1941, lacked telephone facilities and this created enormous problems when it was necessary to make contact. In an attempt at improving communication the Home Office was asked to install a Police Wireless System in Caernarvonshire.

"...Home Office to arrange for three fixed station receivers and transmitters ... at Headquarters (Caernarvon), Conway and Pwllheli and four medium frequency receivers and four transmitters for the patrol cars. The cost of this will be approximately £500..." [GAS XM 1388/163, 162]

The police were expected to arrest enemy parachutists 'as soon as they landed':

"...to be questioned for name and find out if he is a member of the armed forces of the enemy. No detailed interrogation is to be carried out by you. Prisoner to be held in rigorous custody if possible by an armed guard ... if you have any reason to think that the prisoner is a parachutist or saboteur or a member of the enemy armed forces in disguise you will remove everything from him including his clothing ... question him as to his identity, destination ... and make arrangements with MI5 to dispatch an interrogating officer or to give instructions as to the disposal of the prisoner..."

To assist the police in such duties:

"... bloodhounds may be made available for the tracking of missing parachutists etc ... The hound will have to come some distance but will travel in a fast car; part of the training of these particular hounds has been a journey by motor car in order that the hounds may associate travelling in a car with serious work..."

When it came to identifying enemy agents the following points were made:

"...a clear and new Identity Card; clothing of a foreign cut; new tabs on old clothing; address written in continental fashion; possession of a large sum of money; foreign accent but many aliens in this country; lack of knowledge of the neighbourhood; possession of large scale maps; check ration card against Identity Card for consistency; check on

passport (any issued in Luxembourg should be regarded with the gravest suspicion and reported at once to HQ)..."

An allowance of 9d was made for each meal (breakfast, dinner and tea) supplied to prisoners in police custody in Caernarvonshire but this was increased to 1/- for each meal during the war.* [GAS XJ1234/11]

If any part of the country had been invaded the police were told to obey instructions given to them by the 'competent military authority'. Their role was to control the civil population and take precautions against espionage and sabotage etc. and to prevent petrol or other materials falling into enemy hands. Because of the fear of bacteriological sabotage, any leaflets, parachutes etc. dropped on this country were "...to be sent immediately... to the Emergency Public Health Authority Laboratory at Conway for examination..." [GAS XM 1301/5]

The places in Caernarvonshire which were described as being most at risk at the beginning of the war were the Conwy Tubular Bridge, Penrhos Aerodrome, North Wales Power Station at the Dolgarrog Aluminium Works, Petrol Storage Tanks Caernarvon, BBC Studios Bangor, North Wales Power Station Cwm Dili, railway stations and water works. [GAS XJ1234/11]

It was the duty of hoteliers and boarding house keepers to keep a strict record of everyone staying at their establishment. Failure to do so could result in the police prosecuting the culprit. Such a case was brought against the licensees of various places in Bangor where aliens were staying but full particulars had not been recorded. Eleven Dutchmen and one Belgian were discovered to be staying at the *Railway Hotel* in Bangor and solicitors acting on behalf of the hoteliers stated that they were diamond cutters. [*North Wales Chronicle*]

In the Police Aliens Day Book for Caernarvonshire covering the period of the war, a variety of people were recorded as passing through the town of Caernarvon and they included circus performers of various nationalities at the Pavilion, an American carrying out missionary work in Caernarvon as well as Russians, Argentinians, Egyptians, Iraqis and Turks. What is surprising is that 128 Germans, excluding Austrians, were recorded in the town's Police Alien Book during the war. [GAS XJ1469]

The 3rd Bn, Caernarvon Home Guard were able to form a brass band with E W Hughes as bandmaster, Owen E Owen as his deputy, E H Williams as secretary, Corporal R Parry as librarian and E W Hughes as president. There were twenty two bandsmen when it was formed in 1942 and band practices were held on Wednesday nights at 7pm in the Drill Hall, Caernarvon. The first public appearance was on Remembrance Sunday 8 November 1942 when they performed at 10am in Llanrug and 2pm at Caernarvon. [GAS 1301/28]

CHAPTER 5: National Gallery and Manod Quarry

It was not only young children and their mothers who gave cause for concern in time of war. There were also considerable fears that priceless treasures housed in the major cities might be lost forever in the event of aerial bombardment. Consequently, plans for the removal of works of art from London galleries and museums in the

---

* a Prisoner of War who escaped from a working party in Lymm, Cheshire managed to get as far as Bethesda where he was caught by the police. [*NWC* 12.10.45] whilst another managed to steal a yacht at Conwy but was caught ten miles off the coast of the Isle of Man and brought back to Beaumaris [*C&DH* 5.10.45]

National Gallery paintings in storage in the Eagle Tower at Caernarfon Castle. [National Gallery]

National Gallery paintings in storage at Plas y Bryn, Bontnewydd. [National Gallery]

One of the National Gallery paintings being loaded on to an LMS lorry for transfer from the Pritchard Jones Hall at UCNW, Bangor to Manod Quarry. [National Gallery]

The Van Dyke painting of 'Charles I on Horseback' being moved from Penrhyn Castle, Bangor for transfer to Manod Quarry. The LMS low-loader lorry has white-edged mudguards to assist other road users during the blackout.
[National Gallery]

The lorry carrying the Van Dyke painting passes under the Ffestiniog Railway arch. The road beneath the bridge was specially lowered to accommodate the height of this particular painting.
[National Gallery]

The Van Dyke painting approaches Manod Quarry with the quarry sheds to the right.
[National Gallery]

A rail car used for transporting paintings at the entrance to Manod Quarry. [National Gallery]

National Gallery paintings being unpacked at Manod Quarry. [National Gallery]

Mr Holder, National Gallery picture restorer, at work in his studio at Manod Quarry. [National Gallery]

Staff employed by the National Gallery at Manod break for tea. [National Gallery]

event of a war had been under discussion since 1933 when the Rt. Hon. Ormsby-Gore MP (later Lord Harlech), the first Commissioner of Works, called together the directors of libraries, museums and art galleries in the capital. As a result of these discussions a list of country houses and other repositories where such material could be removed for safety was compiled.

With increasing tension in Europe and the possibility of war, ten institutions including the National Gallery applied for space in the National Library of Wales at Aberystwyth. To test the feasibility of the plans which the National Gallery had made, two loads of pictures were sent from London at the time of the Munich crisis but were returned unpacked when the government reached agreement with Germany.

The first intimation of a plan to move the National Gallery pictures from London to Bangor in the event of war came with Mr Kenneth Clark's (later Lord Clark) letter of 30 September 1938 to Mr E H Jones, Registrar of the University College of North Wales (UCNW).

> "Now that the chances of our having to use the Hall at Bangor University as a storage for our pictures have considerably diminished I must write to thank you and the University Authorities for your generous offer to let us use this Hall ..."

This matter was considered so confidential by the college authority that no reference was ever made in the Council Minutes to the subject.

A letter from Mr F I G Rawlins, Scientific Advisor to the Trustees of the National Gallery in Trafalgar Square on 4 November 1938 stated:

> "... should our plans for the dispersal of pictures in Wales ever have to be put into operation it would seem that Bangor would be an ideal place..."

Further confirmation of the availability of the UCNW was sent on 19 February 1939 to the First Commissioner, Office of Works:

> "... the UCNW has placed at the disposal of the National Gallery in the event of war for the purpose of picture storage the Pritchard-Jones Hall...."

On the advice of the Air Ministry, the Trustees decided that Wales would be the safest place for the irreplaceable National Heritage, and around 6,000 pictures were moved out of London. Rail transport was provided by LMSR to Bangor and GWR to Aberystwyth and between 23 August, when the first container load left Trafalgar Square, and 2 September 1939, the whole operation had been completed thus averting possible danger from bombing whilst in transit.

Having arrived safely at their destination, problems then arose with the transportation of the pictures from the respective railway stations to their eventual repository, especially as far as the larger ones were concerned. It was necessary to take into consideration the size of doors, passages or even windows in order to gain access to buildings. Although the main task was to house the pictures the matter of suitable atmospheric conditions had also to be considered.

As far as Bangor was concerned, the Pritchard Jones Hall, because of its size and the fact that it was heated by coke fired boilers, caused problems as regards maintaining anything approaching a constant level of heat. The situation was further exacerbated by the temperature variation between the severe winter of 1939-40 and the unusually hot summer of 1940.

Access to the Pritchard Jones Hall had been difficult but this was not a problem at Penrhyn Castle where there were wide doors into the garages where the larger pictures were to be stored, while other pictures were kept in the castle dining room. Where variations in temperature and humidity presented problems, fans were used to circulate air but where humidity continued to be a problem it was not unknown for old wet blankets and wet felt to be used!

Although Bangor was unlikely to be bombed it was felt that there was some vulnerability since it lay on the route of the German bombers targeted on Liverpool and the north west of England. A letter dated 26 November 1940 to the Ministry of Works, *Palace Hotel*, Rhyl refers to a machine-gun mounted on the College tower for the defence of the building.

Further storage was made available on the lowest floor of the Eagle Tower at Caernarvon Castle which had been adapted to take twenty of the more important pictures, with a similar number stored at a private house, Plas y Bryn, Bontnewydd. However, Samuel Courtauld, as Chairman of the Gallery Trustees, was still concerned for the safety of the pictures and considered an underground shelter to be more suitable.

Around 1,000 pictures from the National Gallery were sent by rail to the National Library of Wales at Aberystwyth for storage in the underground tunnel which had been constructed near the Library between August 1938 and October 1939. It continued in use until May 1945 when the last of the deposited items were withdrawn. Other pictures were deposited at Aberystwyth from the Royal collection at Hampton Court and from a Dutch museum.

During the summer of 1940, owing to the difficulty in supervising different locations and the ever present danger from bombing, it was decided to find a more secure location and various railway tunnels and caves were checked and found to be unsuitable because of difficult access and the possibility of flooding. The National Gallery decided that Manod Quarry, 1,750 feet above sea level in the mountains near the town of Ffestiniog, could be adapted to their needs since, with its 200-300 feet of slate protection overhead, it was considered safe from air attack. The road to the quarry was far from ideal and 5,000 tons of slate rock were removed when the entrance to the quarry was increased in size from 6' x 6' to 13' 6" x 10' which allowed lorries loaded with pictures to be driven inside and so be unloaded unobtrusively.

Each of the six chambers built within the cavern was controlled by a mini sub-station where a plenum unit was installed. The warm air generated by this equipment and controlled by thermostats, was drawn into each chamber by fans. The fans ensured four changes of air per hour in each of the buildings within the quarry which inhibited the growth of mould. The atmosphere within the units was maintained at 65°F and 42% humidity. As an additional precaution, an axial-flow fan was installed adjacent to the tunnel entrance to extract any possible dust from the air.

Since certain paint material such as oil and tempera react to the lack of light, a certain level of illumination had to be maintained in the quarry at all times. The wisdom of installing a 150hp Crosseley diesel engine with a 90kw alternator as a precaution against failure of mains electricity power supply was proved on many occasions when wintry conditions caused an interruption in the mains supply from the North Wales Power Co.

In the summer of 1941, nine months after commencing work, the Ministry of Works announced that Manod Quarry was ready for occupation. Thereafter, it was a matter of conveying the pictures from the six repositories in Wales to Manod. The LMSR was responsible for bringing to the quarry the articles from the Bangor area (a journey of 40 miles) and the GWR from Aberystwyth (a distance of 70 miles). In both cases they were conveyed in containers on lorries.

The first pictures arrived at Manod on 12 August 1941, where all the pictures could be properly supervised and stored in a controlled atmosphere which was to prove far superior even to that at the National Gallery itself. The collection held at the National Library had all been removed to the quarry by September 1941.

The movement of the these container lorries, which were arriving at a rate of three a day, had to be carefully programmed to prevent a clash with empty ones on the narrow four mile road leading to the quarry. Although 600 to 700 pictures were arriving each week, the only problem to arise was with Van Dyke's 'Charles I on Horseback' and Piombo's 'Raising of Lazarus' when it was found necessary for the road beneath a bridge near Ffestiniog to be lowered by two and a half feet to enable the lorry carrying the pictures to pass underneath.

The National Gallery staff stationed at Manod Quarry consisted of the Head Attendant, Mr E B Harrison and 14 men under his charge. Such a number being required because the site had to be guarded night and day. Extra men were also required to move the pictures when necessary. The remoteness of Manod was an advantage since it was away from prying eyes, but problems did arise in wintertime when staff and administrators had to be transported to the nearest village three miles away.

Although the artificial atmosphere created was conducive to the storage of the pictures, it caused problems with the rock roofs. The possibility of a roof fall occurring within the slate caverns was always there and regular checks were made. Paradoxically, the inevitable slate dust had no damaging effect on the pictures but had the pictures remained in London some would have been irretrievably lost when the National Gallery was badly damaged by bombs in 1940.

Manod was retained by the Government for many years after the war because of a possibility of another war particularly during the Cuban missile crisis.

CHAPTER 6: Navy, Army and Air Force Stations

A mountainous coastal area such as North Wales, sited well away from large, heavily populated centres, was ideally suited for the location of military training establishments for all three services.

HMS *Glendower* was a naval base outside Pwllheli for training sailors in theoretical gunnery work. It was housed in a holiday camp, built by Mr (later Sir) Billy Butlin, and comprised rows of chalets designated from A - Z, housing 100 officers and 5,000 sailors. The 500 'Wrens' in the camp had their own billets, well guarded from the remainder of the camp. Among the many officers who passed through the camp was HRH Prince Philip who undertook part of his naval training there.

There were numerous areas taken over by the army as training grounds. The 46th (Liverpool Welsh) Royal Tank Regiment, formed in the spring of 1939, was stationed at Llandwrog, on the outskirts of Caernarvon, during the summer and autumn of 1940. As well as training on Matilda tanks at nearby Glynllifon, they were given the task of guarding the southern entrance to the Menai Strait during the invasion scare of that year.

Another training area was the No. 1 Battle Camp, located at Capel Curig, where Officer Cadets Training Units (OCTU) from Sandhurst were given practical experience of firing live ammunition and participating in military exercises having learnt the theory within a classroom. At one stage this was under the command of Major E L

Kirby who had completed a tour of duty in the Middle East.

The camp headquarters was housed in the *Royal Hotel* (now Plas y Brenin) which had previously been the duplicate HQ of the Searchlight and Anti-aircraft Guns for Liverpool (a unit which would have come into operation immediately if the main operating HQ had been incapacitated by enemy action). When it was decided in March 1943 that the duplicate HQ was no longer required because of reduced air raids on Liverpool, No. 1 Battle Camp was given permission to take over the premises. The staff and cadets were housed in the main building whilst the stables and Nissen huts on the other side of the road housed three Bren Gun Carriers, various machine guns and tons of ammunition.

Officer Cadets arrived by train at Betws y Coed station where they were met by the station master and the Camp Commandant. It was not unusual to find an occasional fishing rod and shot-gun amongst the equipment being carried by the cadets, however, any thought of a holiday was soon dispelled!

The cadets, who were entirely self-sufficient, would participate in exercises – which sometimes lasted for four or five days – in various parts of the mountain depending on the area allocated to them by the Officer Commanding the area, Colonel Ivor Davies (Welch Regiment), based at Llanberis. To make the exercise as realistic as possible the cadets would be 'ambushed' without prior warning to see what their reaction, if any, would be especially when live ammunition was fired in their direction.

Although there were many other training camps in the area, such as the OCTU battle camp at Barmouth, there was virtually no contact between them since travelling was governed by a strictly controlled petrol allowance. The Advance Handling and Field Craft School at Llanberis had various wings including a section called Lovat Scouts (named after Lord Lovat who led the raid on Dieppe) who were considered to be among the forerunners of the modern 'Special Forces' units. One of the instructors at this school was Lieutenant Tasker Watkins (Welch Regiment) who was later awarded the Victoria Cross in Normandy. The Welsh Guards were stationed at Henllys Hall, Beaumaris and at nearby Baron Hill, the Royal Irish Fusiliers were in residence until the Royal Artillery arrived to carry out Search and Direction Finding Courses. The Intelligence Corps also occupied Baron Hill for a while.

In addition to the regular army units which trained in north west Wales, there were some 'clandestine' units based in the area. One such unit was designated 'X-Troop' of No. 10 Inter-Allied Commando, under the command of Major Brian Hilton Jones, the son of Dr and Mrs Hilton Jones. He was born in Harlech but moved at an early age to Caernarvon where his father had his surgery. After gaining his BA degree with a double first in modern languages at Caius College, Cambridge, he was commissioned into the Royal Artillery in 1939. He subsequently volunteered and served with No. 4 Commando before being transferred to No. 10 (Inter-Allied) Commando. Inter-Allied Commando was so named as it was composed of a number of different nationalities including French, Belgian, Dutch, Norwegian, Polish, Yugoslav and 'British' (being alien nationalities, i.e. German and Austrian) and commanded by a British officer.

In the late 1930s people anxious to escape persecution from the Nazis had left Germany and Austria and some had come to this country but, at the outbreak of the war, they were interned as enemy aliens. Rather than be incarcerated behind barbed wire for the duration of the war many of the men volunteered to serve in the British army. Initially, many of them found themselves carrying out menial tasks in the Pioneer Corps but when it was decided that a

The wedding of Captain Brian Hilton Jones at Aberdovey, 1943. The bridal party is surrounded by members of X-Troop of No. 10 Commando. [Mrs Edwina Hilton Jones]

Officers of the 6th Cadet Bn., R.W.F. in camp at Holyhead, 1944. [Mr R T Jones]

specialist unit would be formed within No. 10 Commando, there was no shortage of volunteers keen to perform a more useful and active role.

To be considered for this special unit, it was imperative that each member spoke perfect German and had the ability to operate on his own whenever and wherever necessary. Some still had families on the continent and, since particulars of many of the men were known to the Gestapo, it was decided that each one would forsake his real name and be given a new identity. The existence of this new unit was known to but a few and for this reason it was called the X-Troop (and later No. 3 Troop) being part of No. 10 Inter Allied Commando.

Captain Hilton Jones was placed in command of X-Troop and his initial task was to interview each candidate who had already been interrogated and cleared by MI5. On 23 July 1942, those who had been accepted, moved to Harlech where No. 10 Commando was in the process of being formed. On 21 September, No. 3 Troop went to a new location at Aberdovey where they trained independently from No. 10 Commando. Basic training was carried out between October 1942 and September 1943 followed by operational training and actual engagements until September 1945.(No. 10 Commando was disbanded at the end of 1945).

The basic training included night reconnaissance on Cader Idris; assault marches across the Dovey estuary to Plynlimon and back and a 'sabotage' attack on RAF Towyn. Several visits were also made to Bethesda in North Wales for a course on rock-climbing followed by a march with weapons and kit from Bethesda to Penygroes via Ogwen valley, Crib Coch, Snowdon, Rhyd Ddu and the Nantlle range. When the decision was taken to bring No. 10 Commando under one headquarters rather than being scattered as it had been hitherto along the North Wales coast, the troop left Aberdovey on 31 May 1943 for Eastbourne. Lieutenant W Trevor Matthews from Caernarvon joined the troop on 4 December 1943 but on 5 March the following year he was very badly injured when testing a new type of nylon line for abseiling. As a result of this he spent many months in hospital.

Brian Hilton Jones, who had by now been promoted to Major, formed a special unit of men from the troop to carry out pre-invasion reconnaissance raids on the French coast and for these operations he was awarded the Military Cross. For the actual invasion on 6 June 1944, the troop was split into small groups and attached to the various Commandos that took part. Whilst on a night patrol into German forward areas Major Hilton Jones was badly wounded and captured. He was taken to a German Army hospital in Northern France where he was operated on. Shortly afterwards the advancing Allied armies reached the hospital and he was brought back to Britain for further treatment.

The few aircraft seen in Gwynedd during the First World War, flying from local airfields were the forerunners of those that participated in exhibition flights and flying circuses in the 1920s and 1930s. During the same period a gliding club was established on the Lleyn peninsular. Such peace-time activities were enjoyed by most people but the news in 1936 that the Royal Air Force intended building an airfield to house a bombing school at Penrhos, three miles west of Pwllheli, was objected to strongly by the Welsh Nationalist Party even though it was intended that some 500 local people would be provided with work.

Nevertheless, when Penrhos hosted the Empire Air Day on 20 May 1938, it attracted a great deal of attention and people flocked to see the attractions as described by a local paper:

"... (the) programme will include squadron formation drill, thrilling

aerobatics, converging dive bombing, and formation drill by five Westland Wallace machines. A gas attack, defended by fast planes, will also be staged. Finally there will be a fly-past of various types of aircraft including the new Battle and Hampden types...'[NWWN 1938 Mr R E Roberts]

Violation of the Sabbath was also resented by many including the Caernarvonshire County Council which registered its strong opposition to a proposal by the Air Ministry to amend a regulation to allow Air Gunnery and bombing practice at any time of day or night, including Sundays, throughout the year at the RAF bombing range at Hell's Mouth. [C&DH 2.6.39]

However, opinion on the matter varied as expressed in a local paper:

"Sir, If the recent deputation to Parliament succeeds in getting gunfire and bombing practice stopped on Sunday wouldn't it be advisable for the deputation to approach the heads of the totalitarianism states and ask them in case of war not to bomb us on the Sabbath. Wouldn't that be manifestly unfair if we were not allowed to retaliate on that day." [C&DH 7.9.39]

After the construction of Penrhos airfield in 1936, a further seven airfields were constructed in Gwynedd in the following years: Bodorgan, Hell's Mouth (a bombing range and later a Relief Landing Ground for Penrhos aircraft), Llanbedr, Llandwrog, Mona, Towyn and Valley.

RAF Bodorgan, a grass airfield in south-west Anglesey, had its name changed to Bodorgan from its original name of Aberffraw on 15 May 1941 to eliminate postal and rail delays and the related general confusion which had been experienced. It was opened 11 September 1940 and occupied by 'Z' Flight of 1 Anti-Aircraft Co-operation Unit (AACU) which flew Queen Bee, a radio controlled version of the Tiger Moth, for test shoots by AA gunners at the Ty Croes range. The first radio controlled flight was made on 2 December 1940 with the aircraft eventually crashing on landing after $2^{1}/_{2}$ hours in the air.

A detachment of Lysanders from 13 Squadron at Hooton Park carried out night flying practice in March 1941 and other Lysanders appeared when the airfield became 15 Satellite Landing Ground (SLG) as a dispersal field for Hawarden's 48 Maintenance Unit (MU). Hurricanes were also flown in and 30 aircraft were stored there by the end of May 1941. Wellington and Swordfish joined the aircraft already dispersed from Hawarden but, after several accidents, it was decided that it would be safer to ferry aircraft back to Hawarden prior to dispatch.

In the following months Dragonfly, Lysander, Henley, Tiger Moth and Magister planes were seen to come and go whilst the radio controlled Queen Bee continued its operation. Many Wellingtons were received in 1942 but the total number of aircraft at any one time was maintained at about 30 to prevent them becoming too tempting a target to enemy aircraft which regularly flew over the area on their way to attack Liverpool and the north-west.

During the winter months, when the muddy conditions precluded locally based planes from operating, other local airfields with improved runways were used. By the end of 1944 dispersal of aircraft was no longer necessary and in order to consolidate its activities Hawarden took over Hooton Park as a sub-storage site and, consequently gave up its SLGs.

Bodorgan was closed for flying on 30 September 1945 and returned to agriculture. The two Bellman and one Blister hangars were dismantled but some of the huts are still in use for light industry. There was never a control tower erected but a bungalow-type building was used as a watch office.

Two views of crashed Avro Anson Mk Is at RAF Penrhos, 1939. The silver paintwork on the aircraft was typical of the pre-war peacetime RAF colours. This type of aircraft was commonplace in the area throughout the war years and beyond. As late as the 1960s, an Anson was flying from RAF Llanbedr. One such aeroplane, badly in need of restoration, is on display at the Caernarfon Air Museum.
[Mr R E Roberts]

Aircrew at RAF Penrhos, c1940-41.
[Mr R E Roberts]

4ASR (Air Sea Rescue) launch 1502, RAF Marine Section, Pwllheli, 1941. This RAF unit was housed on the dunes between South Beach and Gimblet Rock, a site now occupied by Partington's boatyard. The boats were built at the Western Marine boatyard, Pwllheli (now Firm Helm). [Mr R E Roberts]

Corporal Ted Roberts (of Pwllheli) with a Lewis gun at RAF Marine Section, Pwllheli, 1941. [Mr R E Roberts]

Crew of the RAF Marine Section, Pwllheli, 1941. [Mr R E Roberts]

RAF Llanbedr: When this base was opened on the Merioneth coast south of Harlech on 15 June 1941, it was intended to be under the control of Valley airfield and with a similar role of guarding the Irish Sea from enemy air operations and providing cover for the convoys. However, the first aircraft there were six Ansons used for training. By October they had been replaced by Spitfires of 74 Squadron (and later 131 Squadron) which took on the role of patrolling the Irish Sea.

After the Spitfires, Llanbedr played host to a variety of other planes including Lightnings, Mustangs, Thunderbolts and Typhoons.

The Lysanders in residence in the early part of 1943 were used by the 2025th USAAF's Gunnery Flight for bombing practice on to a target off the nearby coast.

Squadron Leader William Ross Jones, brought up at Abererch near Pwllheli, joined the RAF in 1929. After training as a Wireless Operator/Navigator, he saw active service in Iraq, Palestine and India. He returned to this country in 1936 to take an Air Observer's course followed, a couple of years later, by qualifying as a pilot. As a Spitfire pilot during the Battle of Britain in the summer of 1940, every day seemed a series of aerial battles with little if any respite until their persistence won the day. Squadron Leader Jones was posted to Llanbedr airfield in 1942 for a tour of duty which involved flying to meet US B24 and Liberator bombers off the coast of Ireland, and guiding them on the remainder of their flight from the USA to Valley airfield.

On 12 March 1942, RAF Llanbedr claimed its first aerial victory of the war when, appropriately enough, a Welshman, Flight Lieutenant Ray Harries, a flight commander in 131 Squadron, shot down (in conjunction with another pilot) a Ju88 which was seen to crash into the sea about 35 miles west of the airfield. Harries went on to become the top Welsh fighter pilot of the war with an official score of 20$\frac{1}{4}$ victories.

Work commenced on RAF Llandwrog, 4 miles SW of Caernarvon, in September 1940 and material for the work was brought in through Caernarvon harbour:

> "... part of the Fletcher and Dixon yard at Victoria Dock to be let to the British Asphalt Co ... for the production of asphalt to cover the airodrome (sic) at Dinas Dinlle –10,000 tons required..."
> [Harbour Trust Minutes 4.2.41]

The Airspeed Oxfords, which were the first planes to arrive at Llandwrog when the airfield was opened 7 July 1941, were there in a defensive role but when the decision was taken that the airfield would be used as the No. 9 Air Gunners School of Flying Training Command, the aircraft were replaced by twin-engined Armstrong Whitworth Whitley bombers.

The airfield was described as a 'dispersed' type with the service personnel accommodated in Nissen huts on the northern end of the main runway so as to be near the aircraft whilst the trainees lived in huts (no. 2 site) on the coast road close to Dinas Dinlle beach. Their day started at 6.40am and, after some physical training, they, and other airmen from various parts of the airfield, were collected by two old ex-Liverpool Corporation buses which took them via the coast road and Llandwrog village to the central communal site which included the officers, sergeants and airmen's mess as well as the post office. On the other side of the Llandwrog to Saron road were the RAF hospital and the WAAF section opened on the 12 September 1942. When the new road was built in 1942 between the airfield and the communal site it enabled the airmen to cycle between the two places.

Llandwrog's blackest day happened on 10 October 1941 when two Whitley aircraft having carried out an exercise were coming in to land. The first one had completed his five mile radius approach and was approaching the runway when the other plane banked to carry out a similar approach and his wing cut off the tail of the first causing it to crash on its nose and burst into flames. The fire was tackled by Cpl. Wilson and his fire-fighting team who also had the dreadful task of removing the bodies from both aircraft. Although the second Whitley also crashed it did not catch fire but, nevertheless, a total of seventeen airmen were killed, including two senior pilots, Sq. Ldr. Barker and Fl. Lt. Martin. Twelve of those killed were buried in their home town and five at Llanbeblig churchyard, Caernarvon.

For the early intake of potential Air-Gunners posted to Llandwrog for training during the severe winter of 1941-42, the airfield seemed anything but hospitable, especially to those men brought from Bangor station in the back of a cold and draughty RAF lorry. The mixture of days of snow and frost followed by rain and sleet, together with wild roaring gales reduced the uncompleted airfield to flooded fields and thick mud. Taking off and landing were only possible because of the concrete runways. It was during this same wintry period, that Les Sidwell, a trainee Air Gunner/Pilot Officer (later to be involved with the Wooden Horse POW escape from Stalag-Luft III) describes how he and other trainees waiting in the crewroom for the weather to improve were taken by surprise:

> "... a German JU88 flew in at sea level without warning and, before the camp defences could open up their guns, damaged two grounded Whitleys and a beacon with cannon fire. It disappeared seawards just as quickly as it appeared..."

When the weather allowed, flying would be carried out in obsolete Whitley bombers which flew along the coast allowing their air-gunners to shoot at drogues towed by Lysanders from RAF Valley. The Whitley was armed with Vickers machine guns housed in turrets and the task of the three potential air-gunners, each one allocated one hundred rounds of ammunition with different colours, was to hit the drogue. Trainees were also taken by ex-Liverpool Corporation buses to RAF Penrhos and then to Hell's Mouth to practise on ground turrets by firing at moving targets. Owing to the heavy snowfall during January 1942 the course, which normally ran for six weeks, was extended to ten weeks.

Les Sidwell's first training venture ended in an unexpected manner:

> "... in January (1942) my first Whitley (Mark V aircraft N1475) flying exercise ended when engine failures out at sea caused the pilot (F/O Watson) to aim for the nearest land, near the golf links by the headland near Morfa Nevin where we crash-landed. We walked to the nearby Linksway Hotel where the splendid Reginald and Dorothy Lane welcomed us and magically whipped up a lovely hot Sunday dinner for us..."

To relieve the monotony of flying up and down Caernarvon Bay on gunnery exercise, the trainees would occasionally get the pilot to fly low over Caernarvon and whilst passing over Castle Square the opportunity was taken to dispose of spent cartridges out of the rear turret which would descend like hail on to the long-suffering inhabitants down below. Inevitably such an incident was reported by the County Constabulary to the Commanding Officer who would reprimand the trainees for their behaviour.

When No. 9 Air Gunners School was closed at Llandwrog on 13 June 1942 it was transferred to RAF Penrhos. Thereafter, Llandwrog became a satellite to Penrhos and served as a Relief Landing Ground for 9 (Observers) Advance Flying Unit based at Penrhos until Llandwrog took over the unit on 11 February 1943. The Whitley bombers were replaced by twin-engined Blenheim fighter bombers, of both the long and short nosed types, for training navigators and wireless operators and then, during 1943, by twelve twin-engined Avro Ansons used for training navigators by both day and night. Many of the Royal Air Force Observer or Navigator air crew had been trained under two schemes described as the Empire Air Training Scheme and the British Commonwealth Training Scheme but, on returning to this country from Canada, the opportunity was then given for them to become familiar with local flying conditions at Llandwrog and Penrhos.

The front at Dinas Dinlle was accessible to the public only for a certain distance along the coastal road towards the airfield and sentries and barricades would prevent anyone going any further. The public was precluded from most of the seaside by coils of barbed wire which extended all the way from one end of the beach to Fort Belan; only occasional gaps would allow the hardy and the brave access for swimming. The barbed wire served to both inhibit any possible invaders and to protect anyone from straying into the mines laid along the shore and publicised at intervals of 20 yards or so with notices in English and Welsh stating "DEATH – HEAVILY MINED". The occasional dog or rabbit killed by exploding mines when it strayed through the barbed wire on the shore, would emphasise the danger.

The coastal sand-dunes bordering the airfield were also defensively mined but when a visiting Mitchell aircraft ran out of tarmac on the main north to south runway and ended up in the minefield it did not cause any of the mines to explode. The airmen who had the task of towing it and the crew back on to the runway, had to crawl along the tyre marks to attach towing gear. A similar incident occurred when a Wellington bomber over-ran the runway and landed in the minefield but again without causing any mines to explode.

Pilot of Spitfire EN851/D Lima Challenger *of 317 Fighter Squadron, USAAF, preparing for take-off at RAF Valley.*
[Mr Dennis Pritchard]

1st Lt Richard Steck (centre leather jacket) briefing crew and passengers before taking off for the USA from RAF Valley, 1945. The aircraft Monotonous Maggie *was a Consolodated Liberator bomber. RAF Valley was used as a transit airfield for aeroplanes returning to the USA at the end of the war in Europe.*
[Mr Dennis Pritchard]

328th BS, 93rd Bomb Group Liberator with twenty sick GIs on board, taking off for the USA from RAF Valley.
[Mr Dennis Pritchard]

In an obviously posed picture, Glory Be, *a USAAF Liberator is about to take off from RAF Valley en route to the USA.*
[Mr Dennis Pritchard]

Entertainment for the airmen usually entailed a visit to one of the three cinemas or a dance at Caernarvon, the journey being accomplished usually by bicycle which was left, with many others, in the safekeeping of Miss Ellis who had a suitable yard off Palace Street.

Although the catering on the airfield had a good reputation, hunger and the need for some warmth caused many of the men to visit nearby families as Les Sidwell described:

"...Mrs Williams' farmhouse [Rhydfelen] was unusually placed on an RAF aerodrome and this good lady's kitchen and parlour provided a haven of warmth and good food in the bitter spells that we had. I was one of the regulars who were glad to warm right up before facing the thought of our billets which were often frozen or swimming in water in the floods..."

Other eating places were the *Harp Inn* in Llandwrog kept by Miss Griffiths, the *Goat Inn* and Albert Lloyd's bakery shop at Llanwnda. The local food supply was supplemented by an abundance of rabbits which overran the sand dunes around the airfield.

When the 1,000 bomber raids started 31 May 1942 three pilots and three Wireless Operators/Air-Gunners from Llandwrog No. 9 AGS instructional staff flew in three Whitley bombers from the airfield: N1345 (P/O D G Box and Sgt. K Houldcroft), T4155 (F/Sgt. K R Rees and Sgt W H Orman) and N1428 (P/O J W Croudis and Sgt. A J Harvey) and they operated out of Driffield airfield during the operation. Whitley N1345 was shot down but the other two planes returned to Llandwrog.

Llandwrog airfield, which was closed on 29 July 1945, was reopened as Caernarvon Airport in 1975, and the flying control tower, previously used by the Royal Air Force, now takes care of civilian planes, whilst the nearby air museum exhibits various memorabilia.

Since the First World War the airfield which bears the name RAF Mona has been variously known as Heneglwys and Llangefni and later Airship Station Anglesey. When it was opened in December 1942 under 25 (Armament) Group it was known as RAF Mona and used as No.3 Air Gunners School flying Blackburn Botha, Fairey Battle and Miles Martinet aircraft followed by Avro Ansons of No. 8 (Observer) Advance Flying Unit from November 1943 to June 1945. Today it is a satellite airfield for RAF Valley and is used for 'circuits and bumps' and for private flying.

After the Air Ministry purchased seven farms at Porth Neigwl on the Lleyn Peninsula and a farm of 250 acres near the village of Penrhos, 500 men started work on excavating and levelling the ground on 21 February 1936. The airfield, known as RAF Penrhos, was opened on 1 February 1937 with an aircraft establishment of six Westland Wallace planes. Three miles away, a marine section (later to be called No. 51 ASR Marine Craft Unit) comprising of five patrol boats was established at Pwllheli with personnel accommodated at the *Victoria Hotel*. The first commanding officer, Wing Commander T V Lister, was also responsible for the target range located at Hell's Mouth, ten miles from Penrhos.

On 1 April 1938, Penrhos was redesignated No. 5 Armament Training Station but at the outbreak of the war it became No. 9 Air Observers School and Wing Commander J J Williamson assumed command. On 1 November 1939 the station became No. 9 Bombing and Gunnery School (B&GS) but by 14 June 1941 it had reverted to No. 9 Air Observers School. A special armament course began on 20 October for fifteen Air-Observers (Navigators) who had been in the USA under the Empire Air Training Scheme. No. 60 Air Gunners Course, the last to be trained at Penrhos, passed out 25 November 1944.

The grave of New Zealander Pilot Officer K P Hamilton at St Denio's Church cemetery, Pwllheli. He was one of five aircrew killed when two Fairey Battle aircraft from RAF Penrhos collided above Rhydyclafdy. [Author's Collection]

The airfield was attacked by enemy aircraft on five occasions, the first one on 9 July 1940 resulted in two officers receiving fatal wounds from fragmentation bombs. Three blocks of officers' quarters were destroyed and two Henley planes (L3290 and L3359) of No. 1 AACU wrecked and a hangar damaged. Although part of the station was subsequently camouflaged a further attack occurred five weeks later when another lone plane dropped bombs and machine-gunned the camp from 200 feet injuring five airmen as well as damaging buildings and vehicles. The raids on 3 and 4 October with bombs and incendiaries being dropped on the latter day inflicted considerable damage but no casualties. As a result of further attacks on 9 and 10 October six Spitfires of No. 611 Squadron arrived from Ternhill as a protective measure but no further attacks occurred.

RAF Towyn, on the Merionethshire coast, flew Queen Bee and Hawker Henley for No.1 Anti-aircraft Co-operation Unit between its opening in August 1941 and closure in May 1945 also Westland Lysanders for No.6 Anti-aircraft Co-operation unit from February 1942 to October 1942. Because it was low-lying there was an inclination for the airfield to flood causing obvious problems for aircraft landing and taking off especially during winter time and so Llanbedr airfield was used instead.

1465 Squadron Air Training Corps cadets and officers at Caernarfon County School, c1945. [Mr Meurig Williams]

The author's Air Training Corps Cadet's Flying Log showing one 2¹/₂ hour flight in Avro Anson EP937 from RAF Mona to the bombing range off the coast at Pwllheli. [Author's collection]

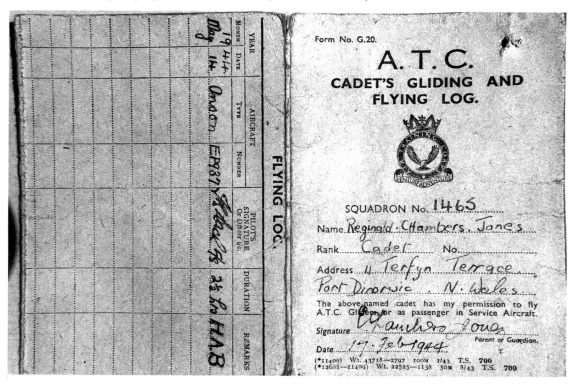

RAF Valley was opened on 1 February 1941 and became operational on 3 March 1941 as RAF Rhosneigr but its name was changed to Valley the following month when it became a Fighter Sector Station under 9 Group Fighter Command with the main task of providing cover for shipping in the Irish Sea and towns and cities in the North West. The first aircraft to arrive on 3 March were Hurricanes from 312 Squadron but these were replaced by similar planes from 615 (County of Surrey) Squadron. Beaufighter aircraft were used by 68 and 219 Squadrons when night operations were started from Valley. Detachments from both the Royal Australian Air Force and the Royal Canadian Air Force were based at this station for a while.

Owing to the good weather which Valley normally experienced when many other airfields were closed, the runways were extended in 1943 at which time taxiways and hard standings were also constructed in anticipation of the arrival of transatlantic aircraft with the first B-17 arriving on 28 July. Thereafter, Valley acted as the first stop in this country for hundreds of US aeroplanes before they continued their journey to East Anglian bases. When hostilities ceased in Europe, Valley was also used as a transit base for planes being flown back to the USA.

By way of initiating young boys into the procedures and traditions of the Royal Air Force, the Air Training Corps (ATC) was formed 1 February 1941 and some 200,000 eventually joined and were issued with uniforms similar to the RAF. Members of the Corps were given the opportunity of flying and learning some of the basic navigating skills whilst still at school. Such activity did not meet with universal approval however and, although the headmaster, E P Evans, was keen to establish an ATC unit at the County School at Caernarvon, a report made on 9 May 1941 by the Arvon Union of Congregational Churches deplored the action of the Board of Education in allowing county schools and colleges to be associated with militarism. [GAS NWC]

During school holidays, and as part of a week's camp at RAF Llandwrog, two cadets from 271 ATC Colwyn Bay Town Squadron took off on Saturday morning 4 September 1943 in Avro Anson EG278 with aircrew Pilot Officer L A Walker and Warrant Officer Winchester. Soon after take-off the plane crashed at Parkia farm, between Felinheli and Caernarvon killing all four on board. The entry made in the Mountain Rescue Service diary is particularly sad and poignant:

"11.10 am – notified by FCO that an Anson a/c had crashed near

The remains of the tailplane unit of a Heinkel 111-H5 of 12 KG40 on the beach near the West End, Pwllheli after being shot down at 1.35am on 30 July 1942. The aircraft was part of a formation flying from Orleans to bomb the Vauxhall Goods Yard in Birmingham. Three of the crew were killed but the pilot, Dirk Hofkes, and wireless operator, Johann Hehser, survived to become PoWs. The crewmen who were killed were: the observer F. W. Horst Vogt, the engineer, Fritz Grazer, and the air gunner, Heinz Hefete, who were buried at Deinio Cemetery, Pwllheli. Their bodies were exhumed in the 1960s and moved to the German cemetery on Cannock Chase, Staffordshire. The Heinkel was brought down by Wing Commander Wolfe and Pilot Officer Ashcroft (Navigator) flying a Beaufighter (No X8291) of 456 Squadron based at RAF Valley. [Edward Doylerush]

As a result of his Spitfire developing engine trouble, a RCAF pilot was forced to bale out of his aircraft which plunged to earth at Beaumaris, damaging the roof of Gwalia Stores before crashing into 17 New Street. The occupant of the house, Mrs Louie Parry was on the first floor when the aeroplane struck and suddenly found herself on the ground floor from where she was rescued by her neighbours and taken to hospital. The pilot landed uninjured in a nearby tree. This photograph shows the aftermath of the crash on 13 March 1941.
[Mr W Williams]

RAF Mountain Rescue Service, 1943. The figures around the jeep are: (L-R) Corporal Gregory McTigue, Flt Lt Graham, LAC Driver Cummings, LAC Jackson.
[Mr R E Roberts]

RAF Mountain Rescue Service Humber Ambulance with canvas extension, RAF Llandwrog.
[Mr R E Roberts]

Caernarvon – Bangor Road about one mile outside Caernarvon. MR unit reached the scene of crash at Parkia farm 11.35 am. All 4 crew had been killed instantly, the plane having broken up in mid-air. 2 false messages were brought by police, one that another a/c had crashed into straits, 2nd that an a/c had been seen to collide with the above Anson. Reference to base by WT in Humber proved these false & further unnecessary search was prevented. Unit withdrew with bodies to base at 12.30 pm..."

In another tragic incident on 9 September 1943 a cadet of 1340 Rhyl Glyndwr Squadron was at camp at RAF Mona and flew in Anson LV152 of 3 Air Gunnery School (AGS) for exercise off Trevor Point, Lleyn. The aircraft hit a cable used to carry material from the local quarry to the jetty, rolled over and crashed upside down in the sea. Three airmen managed to escape but despite rescue attempts, the cadet and the pilot both lost their lives. Fortunately such tragic events did not deter many other youngsters, including the author, from the thrill and excitement of flying for the first time from local airfields after becoming a member of the Air Training Corps. It was from Mona that the author as a member of the Air Training Corps had his first experience of flying on 14 May 1944 in Avro Anson EP937.

Chapter 7: Air Crashes and Mountain Rescue

The mountainous terrain of Snowdonia, especially when adverse weather prevailed, caused many an aircraft to come to grief and lives to be lost during the war. Many of the airmen who were lost in the crashes were in the area to gain experience in navigating and other aircraft skills but, unfortunately, when compared with present-day aircraft, many of the aeroplanes which were being flown during the 1940s were basic and unsophisticated. Instruments, such as the altimeter, could be notoriously inaccurate in the vicinity of the mountains and compass readings were prone to fluctuate wildly. Possibly the only aid to aircraft flying in the mountains were devices called balloon squeakers used to warn them of high ground and, later in the war, these were placed on mountain summits such as Cwm Silin (generally described as an aircraft graveyard) and Foel Grach.

On 8 April 1940 came the first of many incidents which eventually resulted in the formation of the first RAF Mountain Rescue Team. On that day, Blenheim L9093 from No. 13 OTU Bicester, was reported missing. Next day, the aircraft was found completely wrecked on the summit of Carnedd Llewelyn at 3,000 feet having been flown straight into the side of the mountain while in level flight, killing the crew of four.

There followed a series of crashes in Snowdonia which made it necessary for RAF personnel to search for survivors and aircraft in remote and inaccessible mountain areas. In November 1942, the senior medical officer at Llandwrog wrote

"During the past five months there have been 10 major crashes in the area from the Conway Valley to the Rival Mountains which this SSQ (Station Sick Quarters) has attended, over an area of 40 by 30 miles. Time taken varies from one to three days in the mountains, according to the degree of accessibility. Total time away from the station 15 days, total number of dead 40, total number of injured removed to hospital 8..."

At 9pm on 14 January 1943, Anson EG110 from Llandwrog crashed while on a night navex (navigating exercise) to Shrewsbury and back. Next day a telephone message was received stating that the pilot had made his way to a farmhouse. The Station Medical Officer (SMO) and a party then set out to search for the aircraft while air searches were mounted from both Llandwrog and Valley. The ground

search party gave up at 2 am on the 16th owing to the moon setting and bad conditions on the mountain. After resuming the search at dawn, the wreck was eventually located at 11 am, thirty-nine hours after the crash. Two of the crew were dead and the New Zealand Air Force navigator, seriously wounded.

This incident led to a conference on mountain crashes being held at SSQ Llandwrog where it was decided to allocate a Humber ambulance (the roof of which was later painted with black and yellow bands as a 'further aid to ground parties to "home" by day and to indicate its position to co-operating aircraft') and a radio jeep for field trials in the area between Tal-y-Bont, Conwy and Melynllyn hut and also on Carnedd Llewelyn itself. As a result of these trials, the Mountain Rescue Service (MRS) was started by Fl. Lt. George Graham, Senior Medical Officer at Llandwrog on 6 July 1943 on which day the team was first called out, fully equipped, to attend an aircraft crash. From that time on they were to be called out in all weather conditions and to all sorts of terrain sometimes with rewarding results but, unfortunately, in many cases discovering that the crew had been killed. In August, Wing Commander Ruffell Smith arrived at Llandwrog from HQ Flying Training Command to ascertain the progress being made with the 'Crash Party' or, as it was officially called, the Mountain Rescue Service (MRS). With Smith came Flying Officer Richwaite of the Royal New Zealand Air Force who hoped to learn something of the MRS in order that a similar service could be started by him in New Zealand.

In many instances the MRS had excellent support from local police and hill farmers whose knowledge of the terrain enabled them to assist in locating the scene of a crash. As the result of a report being received by the local police the MRS team were alerted on 18 August 1943 and the resulting diary entry reads:

"23.00 hrs – notified of crash E of Bethesda and N of Llyn Ogwen... all crew dead ... MRS party (F/Lt Graham, Sgt. Harvey, LAC Jackson) ... A/C Ventura ... 20 men to help remove bodies ... a mountain stretcher fitted with sledge runners was loaned from Ogwen cottage & proved extremely useful in carrying bodies over grass and loose rock..."

In some cases, because of difficult terrain and poor visibility, it would take a day or two to discover the crashed aircraft:

"29.8.43 – 17.00 hrs – ... report of a Botha crashed eastern Carnedds (no trace found after a great deal of searching until 31.8.43 when it was seen from an aircraft five miles from purported crash site) ... crew of 4 killed instantly ... bodies tied to stretchers but the severity of the ground delayed the return ... decided to leave the stretchers where they were as the party was considerably exhausted & return in daylight ... 1.9.43 fresh party sent out at 0900 to retrieve bodies...Thus ended the longest continuous operation in which the MR unit had been employed. The long delay in finding the crash was due entirely to have been given a grossly inaccurate pin point..."

When an aircraft ditched in the sea the MRS worked with the Air Sea Rescue service as occurred on 1 June 1944. At ten minutes past one in the morning, when the MO & SSQ staff had retired to bed and were trying to sleep through a heavy thunderstorm with torrential rain and lightning flashes dazzling and continuous, reports were received of an aircraft which had overshot the runway on landing at Llandwrog and had ditched in the sea about one mile off-shore. On being called out the MO (Fl. Lt. Scudamore) together with Sgt. Harvey and Cpl. Jackson established from a small group of airmen on the beach that they had seen the aircraft with its lights on. A few red Very lights had been fired but the aircraft lights disappeared after about 5 minutes. Even the flashes of lightning revealed nothing in that position. The MO had been told that the Air Sea Rescue unit at Fort Belan had been duly notified of the crash and that their pinnace had left base. A dinghy was immediately 'commandeered' from the nearest aircraft available and inflated. After paddling for about 1/2 hour it was seen that the Very lights were being sent up not from the aircraft but from a dinghy launched from the aircraft. The MO boarded it to give the crew a check but decided that no immediate medical aid was required. The two dinghies were lashed together and the MO's party began to row towards the shore where 'one could now see numerous bright lights and masses of people - reminiscent of Blackpool'.

To avoid duplication and wasting time and effort, all reports of crashes were co-ordinated by the Flying Control Officer (FCO) and he invariably notified the Mountain Rescue Unit whenever a crash occurred:

"8.11.43 At 20.55 hrs the FCO notified MRU that a crash had occurred and preliminary reports from HQ 9 Group suggested that it had occurred near Snowdon ... at 2115 the local Observer Corps informed MRS through the FCO that a fire had been seen near Carnedd Dafydd at 20.30. Bethesda police station appeared to have more information so the MO and the crew of MRS left SSQ at 2140 in Jeep and Humber and called at Bethesda Police Station ... established mountain HQ by the side of a farm near Llyn Ogwen...a civilian party with police officers and a small contingent from MU RAF Bethesda ... had just descended from the crash where they had found 4 corpses ... MRS crew ascended and found the a/c at 01.00 hrs. 9.11.43 near the summit of Pen yr Oleu Wen (3210 feet) map ref. 121840 ... The a/c (aircraft) was an Anson (N.9855) from Halfpenny Green ... four dead bodies were found and (later) ... a fifth body ... all five had multiple injuries and must have died instantaneously..."

It was always gratifying to the Medical Officer attached to the MRS when there were survivors from a plane crash as was the case at 12.30 pm 1 December 1943 when Anson aircraft (No. EF909) from Jurby, Isle of Man crashed the previous evening near the summit of Foel Grach. Two members of the crew had walked down from the crash to Bethesda where they were met and questioned by the Medical Officer about the location of the crash but they were vague about it. After searching Carnedd Llewelyn a report stated that the third member of the crew had walked from the crash and arrived at Bethesda police station. Eventually the wreck was found and the fourth crew member was sleeping in the potential gun turret compartment at the rear intact part of the fuselage. He had wrapped himself in a few parachutes and apart from suffering from dehydration, starvation and a fractured foot the report stated that his spirits were high. On being offered rum by the MO he refused it saying that 'he never touched the stuff'. He was conveyed on a stretcher down the mountain-side in darkness and taken to SSQ at Llandwrog.

On 3 January 1944 F/Lt Graham leader of the MRS, who had done a tremendous amount of work in getting the service off the ground, was told to report to "Airways Traffic" London for posting overseas. His duties were taken over by F/O Scudamore. Other medical officers involved with the MRS were Sq/Ldr. Collins, and F/Lt. Lloyd.

There was often a sense of frustration amongst the team if they were not informed quickly of an aircraft crashing. This happened on 7 January 1944 when a Liberator aircraft crashed at 1.45 pm between Llanfairfechan & Penmaenmawr shortly after leaving RAF Valley, Anglesey. The MRS was not notified until 1600 hours by which time civilian ambulances had taken six members of the crew of eleven to the Caernarvonshire and Anglesey Infirmary in Bangor for treatment. Two other injured members of the crew walked over the mountain whilst another was picked up by the MRS at Penmaenmawr. Eventually the MRS reached the aircraft at 5.30 pm and amongst the burning debris found three charred bodies which were removed to the mortuary at Bangor (this incident was also recorded in the Police Journal pp102). [GAS XJ 2366]

Testing of various pieces of equipment took place over a period of time. One such item, the "sledge stretcher" (invented by Dr D G Duff, of Denbigh) which was designed to assist in bringing casualties off the mountain as quickly and as efficiently as possible, was tested in February 1944. Following on modifications which were made to the stretcher, further trials took place in June on the scree on the west face of Tryfan with two types of stretcher, one, an all-steel collapsible type with a detachable wheel and the other a light metal framework designed to clamp over a wooden GS stretcher thereby converting it to a sledge stretcher. A Bergen rucksack and Mk.III Everest cradle which could carry a casualty bag used for keeping a patient warm, were also developed.

To improve the efficiency of the MRS team still further, a two-week course in mountaineering, rock climbing, cross country marching and evacuation of casualties under Sgt. Pick of the 52nd Mountain Division started on 4 April 1944.

When a crash occurred on Craig Ffynnon in the Conway Valley on 21 February 1944 MRS Llandwrog was advised of the event by FCO at 1135 hrs:

"MRS left SSQ at 11.42 am and after calling at Conway police station picked up Police Constable Jones (PC 99) at Tynygroes who guided Humber up appropriate mountain track to a farm house where base was established ... Local farmer stated that there were 3 survivors in the a/c and one killed. MO proceeded immediately towards crash with packset, first aid outfit and a Thomas' splint and was followed by PC Jones & 2 civilians carrying 2 GS stretchers with blankets etc..a few civilians at the crash had kept the survivors warm and one administered tea...The a/c was an Anson LT433 from RAF Cark...The pilot, Sgt Grant, was strapped in his seat ... presume that death was instant-aneous...W/O Redman ... taken to Llandudno & District General Hospital...MO attended to the other two occupants ... They were P/O Byrne, pupil w.op and Sgt Birch, navigator..."

In some cases the role of the MRS was simply to locate aircrew who had baled out of their aircraft as was the case on 29 March 1944:

"MRS having collected crew left SSQ at 1435. Conway police station was reached at 1515 & a civilian then guided the vehicles to a house 2 1/2 miles from Conway overlooking the river Conway. From there the crash could be seen on the east bank of the river. The pilot & one other member of the crew were in the house & gave information that the remaining three of the crew had baled out at 9000 feet three minutes before them. They themselves had baled out at approx. 1000 feet...the remaining three had arrived without injury at Conway police station having landed about 4 miles down the road to Talybont near Caerhun...."

Probably the most dramatic and tragic rescue incident, involving both service and civilian personnel, occurred on 28 August 1941 when, at about 11.30am, a Botha aircraft (L647) crashed into the sea off Rhosneigr at a time when a gale was blowing from the south-west causing a heavy sea. Owing to the Holyhead lifeboat being out of action the Porthdinllaen lifeboat was launched at 12.48pm reaching Rhosneigr at 2.30pm. As soon as the aircraft came down in the sea one member of the crew clung to the fuselage but another two were washed off. Two boys of 17, J Wood of Chester and D Baynham of Walton-on-Thames who had seen this happening launched a dinghy.

It took them three quarters of an hour to reach the aircraft but as they turned to go alongside it the boat was capsized by a wave and they were thrown in the water. Nevertheless they, together with the airman, whom they had persuaded to leave the aircraft, started to

Aerial view of Glyn Rhonwy, Llanberis showing the railway marshalling yard alongside the lake and, above and slightly to the right the bomb storage area where the roof caved in on 25 January 1942. The quarry area where the bulk of the bombs were stored can be clearly seen.   [Gwynedd Archive Service]

The Glyn Rhonwy bomb storage area where the roof caved in during 1942. The two floors of the store can be seen. [Author's Collection]

Some members of staff of 31 MU, Llanberis. [Mrs Margaret Sheldon]

Some members of staff of 31 MU, Llanberis. [Mrs E M Jones]

swim for shore but only managed to reach a beach defence post. The airman was too weak to continue any further so the boys left him clinging to the post as they continued for the shore. By then they were very weak and their plight was seen by people on the shore who made a human chain which reached far enough into the water to rescue them. Although the airman was in his own depth, the struggle had been too much for him and he was swept away from the post and was drowned.

In the meantime, further gallant attempts to rescue the other two airmen were made by four shore boats, and by many people working from the beach, but all the efforts failed, and not only were the three airmen lost, but also eleven of those who had tirelessly attempted to reach the airmen.

With the disbanding of RAF 9 (O) AFU (Satellite) Llandwrog, Flt. Lt. Scudamore was posted to RAF Llanbedr prior to the Mountain Rescue Service being transferred there on 7 June 1945. On the next day an American B17G Flying Fortress, ferrying US personnel home to the United States, crashed near Cader Idris at 1,200 ft. and the MO at Llanbedr was notified by FCO of the crash. The aircraft was found burnt out and 20 bodies were recovered from the debris; most of them having received multiple injuries and burns and had been killed instantly.

After a couple of further entries relating to two training exercises, the diary was signed by Fl. Lt. T O Scudamore and closed on 18 September 1945.

The people involved with the Mountain Rescue Service at Llandwrog and Llanbedr had undoubtedly given a tremendous service, more often than not in very dangerous places and in dreadful weather. Their task was not made any easier with the initial equipment used which was primitive and inadequate. The general issue clothing was totally unsuitable for the task and yet the daunting and often harrowing work was carried out with fortitude irrespective of time of day or night. Undoubtedly, without the persistence and tenacity displayed by the team led by the station Medical Officer, many more crew members would have been lost on the mountains.

CHAPTER 8: Bomb Storage

31 Maintenance Unit

Storage of high explosive bombs and similar devices during times of war presented many problems not least being the danger to the public. The old quarry at Glyn Rhonwy, Llanberis had been chosen in 1939 as a suitable place for a bomb store because of its accessibility by both rail and road and any potential danger to the public could at least be reduced.

When the depot, described as 31 Maintenance Unit and forming part of 42 Group, Maintenance Command [GAS-X/CA/160-169] was opened in May 1941, the first consignment of high explosive bombs of 250 and 500lbs, was brought by rail from a munitions factory in Swindon.

On arrival, such trains were initially shunted into a marshalling yard, situated between the main road and Padarn Lake, before being taken by diesel engine through a tunnel beneath the main road directly into underground storage. Specially constructed sidings, large enough to accommodate eight wagons, allowed the bombs to be manhandled on to nearby platforms before being stored on two floors within the quarry, each floor being roughly the size of a football field, and interconnected by lifts and stairs. The bombs were stored in pyramid fashion with the heavier bombs kept on the ground floor.

Bombs, both incendiary and high explosive, were also stored out in the open at Glyn Rhonwy, stacked and grouped in accordance to their size and weight with each stack seventy five yards apart and covered with a tarpaulin. These open-air sites were designated with names such as Piccadilly Circus, Burlington Square, Clapham Common, Hounslow, Olympic, Sevenoaks etc. and such designations were used on a chart in the administration office as a means of establishing the location of the various bombs. A colour code identified the content and weight of the bomb and this too was recorded on the same chart.

Similar open-air sites were used near the villages of Rhiwlas and Clwt y Bont on the other side of Llyn Padarn and in the old lead mines at Holywell which came under the care of 31 MSU (Maintenance Satellite Unit). Marconi's old radio station building at Ceunant near Llanrug was used to store bomb fins.

Orders for bombs or ammunition were usually received by teleprinter and deliveries were made either by rail or by road depending on the destination, route and possible problems with unloading. When deliveries were taken by Matador or Scammel lorries to various airfields or to Liverpool for shipping abroad, two red flags were displayed on each vehicle to indicate the type of load being carried. When sent by rail, bombs up to 500lbs in weight would be loaded by a gang of men using planks and ropes but those in excess of that figure were moved with the aid of a crane. The sealed wagons were documented with coded tickets which gave no indication of their eventual destination.

On 25 January 1942 disaster struck when part of the concrete roof over the storage area known as the tunnel, collapsed on to 8,230 tons of high explosive bombs. Following on the removal of the debris, the bombs were taken initially to Rhiwlas and Clwt y Bont where they were stored in the open and guarded by the RAF.

In a building described as the belting sheds, which stood near the marshalling yard at Llanberis, women deftly loaded ammunition belts with .303 inch bullets and later 35mm cannon shells for use in fighter aircraft. The loaded belts, containing 1,000 to 1,500 rounds depending on the size of the bullet or shell, were then placed in metal boxes and sealed prior to being put in wooden boxes. Such loading continued for a while after the end of the war.

Possibly the only fatality caused by explosives at Glyn Rhonwy occurred 5 July 1944 when a box of detonators being carried in the proof yard exploded and Mr Ivor David Roberts of Llainwen, Llanberis died from his injuries. Two others, Mr John Parry, Bryngro, Cwmyglo and Mr George Williams, Tyn'n Twll, Waenfawr were injured in the same incident.

Civilian wages were £5 per week in 1945 but an additional 5/- (25p) was paid when an element of danger existed with the work such as checking tins of ammunition for any faults. Although this was an RAF base, most of the duties, during the early years were performed by civilians but, gradually after suitable training, RAF personnel took over the handling of the bombs.

By June 1943 many of the explosives stored at Llanberis had become obsolete or had deteriorated and were no longer required and the opportunity was taken for No. 2 MU of the RAF School of Explosives, a unit which dealt with the destruction of explosives by detonating and burning, to be transferred to Llanberis.

Course No. 41 was started on 27 June 1943 and initially 571 incendiaries of 4lbs and 25lbs were burnt in a nearby quarry specially allocated for the purpose. A further 173,000 25lb incendiaries and 88,000 4lb incendiaries were destroyed between December 1943 and

September 1944 and a further 95 tons of incendiary bombs by the end of that year. At the same time Llanberis was used as a disposal site for obsolete pyrotechnics brought in from throughout the UK by rail.

The explosives, were transferred by gravity fed rollers through a tunnel to a point where they could be dropped down a chute to the quarry floor. There, in theory at least, they would explode and burn harmlessly and cause sufficient fire to dispose of other pyrotechnics which followed down the chute.

Unfortunately, the wind had a habit of changing direction and, when that happened, it was not unknown for the summit of Snowdon to completely disappear in black smoke causing a number of complaints from climbers, walkers and the Snowdon Mountain Railway company. Similar complaints were received if there was a change in the direction of the wind resulting in the smoke being blown towards Fachwen and Brynrefail. Since disposal of the bombs was totally dependent on the weather and the wind in the right direction, every opportunity was taken when it was favourable to dispose of as many explosives as quickly as possible since they only had a certain period of time to complete the job and could only work during daylight hours.

By 1955 Llanberis had become a Maintenance Sub-Unit of RAF Llandwrog and the disposal of detonators, 750 and 1,000lb incendiary clusters, UX bombs, signal cartridges, pyrotechnics and anti-aircraft devices by exploding and burning continued until July 1956. However, although the Unit was closed in August 1956 the problem of the explosive devices which had failed to detonate or burn, still remained (see Appendix 2).

CHAPTER 9: Agriculture

The shipping losses incurred during the First World War because of U-boat action and the shortage of food which resulted, nearly brought about the collapse of the country. Such shortages should have made the authorities realise how dependent the country was on imported food but, rather than develop an efficient agricultural industry during the twenty years between the two wars, 60% of the country's food was still being imported at the outbreak of war in 1939.

A farmer writing in 1931 (*Farmer's Glory*) reflects the feeling of frustration that the industry felt at that time:

"Probably one of the hardest things for farmers to realise today is that they are considered unimportant people by the majority of the community. When the townsman is hungry the food producer is a very important person, but today the consuming public are being fed by foreign countries very cheaply...The zest has gone out of farming...It is not pleasant for a man to discover that he is engaged in an occupation for which his country has neither use nor interest..."

The long hours of work and low wages did nothing to attract workers on to the land and this lack of skilled manpower exacerbated the situation. Almost one half of the land devoted to crops was derelict as were buildings and roads. Much of Welsh farmland had been given over to sheep and cattle breeding. In an attempt to correct the poor state of land the Agriculture Act of 1937 allowed a 50% grant towards the cost of lime, the lack of which was considered to be the major cause for derelict land. Basic slag was plentiful and supplies of other fertilisers were adequate at the start of the war but there were insufficient phosphates to meet the increasing acreage of cultivated land.

Even though names had not been published nor individuals approached, those considered suitable to serve on the War Agricultural Executive Committees (WAEC) had already been selected by the Minister of Agriculture. The Munich Crisis caused the Minister to instruct the Chairmen, Executive Officers and Secretaries and certain other members of the Executive Committees to be prepared to act on receiving further instructions. Activating instructions were received on Sunday 3 September 1939 demanding that the War Committees take immediate action and informing them that they were empowered by the Ministry of Agriculture to enforce wartime measures.

The Anglesey War Agriculture Executive Committee based at the Shire Hall, Llangefni, sent out letters early in September indicating what was required of the farmers:

"... landowners are asked to put all their lands in their occupation and/or lands annually let by them for grazing in a state to produce the maximum of food ... The Minister of Agriculture in his broadcast 4.9.39 mentioned as a round figure that 10% of the grassland in this country should be put under the plough and cultivated for 1940 crops..." (PNP 487).

Each committee was made up of seven unpaid local people connected with agriculture plus two to represent the Women's Land Army (WLA) and agriculture workers. Sub-committees were then formed to deal with specific duties such as cultivation, labour, farmers' requirements, machinery, drainage, finance, feeding stuffs and ploughing. In addition groups of men, four to seven in number, were formed into District or Parish Committees directly responsible to fellow-farmers. The ten members on the Executive Committee usually met once a month and a similar number on the District Committee met bi-monthly. Such regular meetings allowed any problems to be dealt with quickly and efficiently.

Although these members were acting on a voluntary basis they devoted a tremendous amount of time and effort into the organisation and its success was due to their personal farming experience, knowledge of local conditions and empathy with farmers in their district whom they were to guide and assist. The farmers themselves readily accepted such assistance since it was an opportunity for improving the land and making it more productive.

Those who could not plough land as directed by the Executive Committee because they had not the implements to undertake the task or the money to pay for the work to be undertaken on their behalf, usually had their land taken over and ploughed by workers employed by the WAEC. The same course of action was taken if farmers refused on principle to carry out the WAEC's instructions.

The first task at the outbreak of war was to bring in the harvest as quickly as possible so as to clear the fields for action, and get two million extra acres of land ploughed and sown. Such was the sense of urgency that the War Office agreed to the request made by the Ministry of Agriculture for soldiers to assist on the farms at this critical time.

The National Farm Survey called for by the Ministry of Agriculture in 1940 recorded the state of every farm in the country. It had the awesome task of surveying every holding with more than five acres of land with the aid of 6 inch-scale Ordnance Survey maps. Detail had to be recorded of the condition of each farm, the state of the land, the types of soil to be found there, the acreage of crops and of grass, and the areas of dereliction. They had to note also the state of buildings, cottages, cart-roads, fences, ditches, water, if electricity was available and whether the farms were infested with rats, rabbits and other pests. Furthermore, an opinion had to be given as to

War Agricultural Executive Committee, Dolgarrog near anti-tank blocks which, in the event of invasion, would be positioned across the road.
[The late Mr H Vaughan Jones]

Machine Section of the Caernarvonshire War Agricultural Executive Committee, 1943.
[The late Mr H Vaughan Jones]

whether or not the farmer was a good one or not and, if the survey found the land in poor heart, suggestions had to be made of ways of improving it. Such information was used for both immediate needs and future planning.

The Scientific Food Committee appointed by the Lord Privy Seal in July 1940 with its committee under the chairmanship of the President of the Royal Society, had the task of considering and advising upon problems relating to national food requirements and, more especially difficulties arising from reduced imports from abroad of food and animal feeding stuffs which this country had relied upon in the years immediately preceding the Second World War.

The Committee had to establish the minimum food requirements of the people of this country on the assumption that the quantity being imported would get less and less because of enemy action. It had to calculate an individual's basic needs in terms of vitamins, calories, minerals and proteins and also in terms of a worker's requirements. Apart from some fats and wheat which would have to be imported, the Committee was of the opinion that all other foods could be produced at home in sufficient quantities to meet the needs of the whole population provided that milk production could be increased by 20% and potatoes output by 100% together with appropriate increases in other foods. This was the period when the National Growmore fertiliser based on a ratio of 7:7:7 (phosphates, potash and nitrogen) was developed by Government scientists to assist in increasing food production.

The Minister of Agriculture, having decided that an additional two million acres of land had to be ploughed nationwide, would advise the chairman of each County Committee of his quota of additional acreage. Such a quota would in turn be shared between each District Committee and sub-divided even further between each Parish Representative. This last allocation would then be divided between

Caernarvon Young Farmers Club members at Vaynol, near Bangor. [Miss Beryl Owen Jones]

Caernarvonshire War Agricultural Committee, 1945. [The late Mr H Vaughan Jones]

Pwyllgor Amaethu Adeg Rhyfel Sir Gaernarfon, 1945.

PWYLLGORAU DOSBARTH.

| Harry Griffith | Rd. Thomas | Emyr Roberts | E. R. Jones | Ivor Owen | David Jones | S. W. Jones | R. P. Roberts |
| Ll eyn | Lleyn | Lleyn | N. Conwy | Ogwen | Gwyrfai | N. Conwy | Eifionydd |

| W. O. Hughes | Rd. Hughes | Griff. Jones | W. P. Jones | D. P. Williams | John Williams | Robt. Jones | Thos. Jones | J. G. Jones |
| N. Conwy | Lleyn | Lleyn | Eifionydd | N. Conwy | Eifionydd | Eifionydd | Eifionydd | Lleyn |

| D. B. Thomas | E. J. Jones | Wm. Owen | John Jones | E. R. Jones | W. R. Williams | R. Jones-Parry | Ellis Williams | O. T. Hughes |
| | | Cad. Eifionydd | Cad. Lleyn | Pwyllgor Sir | | Cad. Gwyrfai | Cad. N. Conwy | Gwyrfai |

| H. V. Jones | Meirion Jones | D. Owen | Ed. Owen | R. W. Roberts |
| N. Conwy | N. Conwy | Eifionydd | Lleyn | Lleyn |

H. D. Hughes
Conwy

each farmer in his section according to the size of the farm.

To help the committees, the Government provided them with a staff of experts, under an Executive Officer, to supply information about modern farming methods and techniques. Apart from the voluntary, unpaid committee-men who gave up all their spare time to the job, the Ministry of Agriculture had the benefit of the best technicians in the country specialising in a particular branch of husbandry. Also each Executive Committee had a back-up paid office staff of about twelve people, being a mix of youngsters, retired people and technicians.

From a situation where little interest was taken in agriculture, suddenly, because the country was at war, the farmer had at his disposal the free advice and assistance of experts on every conceivable subject.

District Committees would arrange evening 'Fire Side Chats' which took place at designated farms with three or four neighbour farmers being invited along with a speaker from the WAEC, or 'War Ag' as it was generally known, for an informal chat about agricultural matters. These talks were not a recent innovation for it had always been the custom for farmers to gather at different farms and, whilst the men discussed 'official' matters, the wives would be in the kitchen preparing a meal and having their own fireside chat and putting the world to right.

At the start of each year a District Officer, such as the late Griffith Williams of Tyddyn Perthi, Port Dinorwic, with the aid of an Ordnance Survey map would have 'walked the farm' and discussed with the resident farmer which fields were to be cultivated. It was this knowledge of each farm under his control and his close working relationship with the farmer that enabled any disputes to be kept to a minimum. Common sense usually prevailed but if any disagreement arose as to the area to be cultivated, or indeed on any other matter, then it was discussed in the monthly district committee.

When potatoes were planted, a careful note was made by the Cultivation Officer of the acreage involved and the quantity supplied by the Potato Marketing Board more especially since it was virtually impossible to check the quantity actually planted. However, the harvesting of the crop, often carried out with a horse or tractor drawn machine hired from the WAEC, would normally confirm or otherwise if most of the seed supplied had been sown. A suitable proportion of the harvested crop would be retained as seed for the following year (seed potatoes were invariably coloured with a dye to make them less attractive for human consumption and as a means of tracing them).

Such was the demand for additional land that public parks and golf courses, both public and private, were ploughed to increase food supplies. Land between fruit trees was ploughed and potatoes planted. Bracken-covered Welsh hillsides were ploughed and transformed with the aid of caterpillar tractors for reseeding and, when possible, to grow potatoes.

Paradoxically, although there was a desperate need for extra land for cultivation, the Ministry of Defence took over hundreds of acres for training, coastal defences and airfields and during the years between 1939 and 1945, 444 airfields were constructed in the UK. The anti-landing devices placed in large fields to prevent invading planes from landing, would be as much, if not more of a handicap to the tractors working in the fields as they were to a potential enemy.

Early in the war, Lord Anglesey became personally involved with Plas Newydd Home Farm of 223 acres and Plas Newydd Park of 44 acres, as well as the other tenanted farms belonging to the estate. He decided to plough up the Plas Newydd cricket ground in order that winter oats could be sown but, as he had no implements for the work

the WAEC were asked to plough and cultivate it for him. Similarly, he decided to plough the golf course, which covered some 34 acres, and again asked the WAEC to carry out the task but early the following year, he had to inform them that he was not able to plough as much of the golf course as he wished as the military authorities had requisitioned about 8 or 9 acres (PLP 572). In April 1943 Lord Anglesey was invited to become a member of the Anglesey War Agriculture Committee (PLP 572).

If the WAEC considered the method of farming or rate of production to be unsatisfactory they arbitrarily took over the farm in question and this happened with the tenanted farm of Plas Llwynon which they found to be in a "... disgraceful condition, both arable and pasture ... (being) semi-derelict...". As a result the tenant was dispossessed by the WAEC, which held the necessary powers invested in them by the Minister of Agriculture, and the farm was taken over by the owner, Lord Anglesey in 1942.

This also happened at Trefarthin Farm on Anglesey (owned by the Vaynol Estate) as late as 1944. In a futile attempt to have the decision changed, a letter was sent to Miss Megan Lloyd George MP by the farm manager asking her to see the Minister as it was felt that 'a great injustice would be done if the War Agricultural Committee were allowed to take over the farm'. [GAS Vaynol Papers]

The various Government campaigns did everything possible to make the public as well as the farmers aware that every small piece of ground was to be used for growing food. Amongst the many posters appearing were those issued by the Ministry of Agriculture asking the public to "Grow More Food Campaign", "Lend a Hand on the Land", "Dig for Victory" and, as a reminder of the role and risks being taken by Merchant Seamen in bringing food into the country "The Life-Line is Firm Thanks to the Merchant Navy".

During the winter of 1939-40, farmers had the formidable task of ploughing additional land which had been grazed for many years in order that winter frosts could prepare it for the additional crops to be sown. However, this was no easy task because the exodus of agricultural workers into the armed forces or to other industries paying better wages, necessitated alternative farm labour being enlisted. In an attempt at retaining or even attracting agricultural workers, council houses were specifically built for them with the WAEC deciding on their allocation.

Although the main campaign to persuade women to join the Women's Land Army was still to come, the realisation of the need for women to assist on the farms came before war had been declared and by the beginning of 1939 nearly 4000 applications for enrolment in the WLA had reached the Ministry of Agriculture and continued to be received from women in every walk of life and ages ranging 13 to 82! By far, most of them came from women in their 20s and 30s many of whom had already had some experience of work on the land.

When Ernest Bevin, Minister of Labour and National Service, urged women over 20 years to register voluntarily for war work only 300,000 did so nationally. Consequently conscription was applied to both men and single women and mothers with children over fourteen years of age (although women were not called upon to fight) with the Women's Land Army being one of the options. It was estimated that nine out of ten women were eventually engaged in some sort of war work.

A committee was appointed for each county, with local welfare representatives to care for land-girls coming into their district. Although there had been initial reluctance on the part of farmers to employ women on the land, the increasing workload imposed by the War Agricultural Committees, ensured that any prejudice was soon

Womens Land Army at Caernarfon Castle, 1943.
[Mrs Megan Edwards]

Womens Land Army –
Marian Birchall with the
sheepdogs at Plas Tirion
Farm, Llanrug.
[Mrs Mary F Williams]

Womens Land Army – Timber Corps, 1943.
L-R: Nancy Britton, Mary Edwards, Ida Bradshaw,
* Betty Butcher, Megan Edwards.*
[Mrs Megan Edwards]

*American crawler tractor pressing air
out of silage.
[Mr Ivor Wyn Jones]*

*Mr Cledwyn Jones, Plas Llansadwrn,
preparing for bailing.
[Mr Cledwyn Jones]*

*Bailing at Plas Llansadwrn farm, Anglesey.
[Mr Cledwyn Jones]*

Womens Land Army rat catchers, c1945.
L-R: Betty Humphreys, Emily Evans, Megan Williams
[Mrs Betty Williams]

X/Gorddinog/19] Houses such as Plas Glyn-y-Weddw at Llanbedrog and Abergwynant Hall, Penmaenpool were used as hostels for those members who were not living at their place of work.

Marian Birchall was born in Spain and worked at the British Consulate at Barcelona until she and her mother left the safety of a neutral country in November 1942, to fly to Portugal. From there they were able to obtain a passage in a cold and draughty Empire seaplane (Golden Hind) which flew them from Lisbon to Northern Ireland, without the benefit of food or drink on the flight, to land on a lake near Belfast from where they continued their journey to Poole in Dorset. She came to Caernarvonshireso as to be near her brother, who was with the RAF at Llandwrog airfield, and by January 1943 she had joined the WLA.

For many of the recruits training took the form of practical work on the farm but Marian Birchall and others had the benefit of spending a month at Madryn Farm at Aber

"... we had to learn how to milk by hand. Some of us would be milking in the morning and the others in the afternoon. We only milked one cow per day! We also learned about dairy, poultry, garden and farm work..."

From Madryn she was posted to a farm in Dolwyddelan where she worked for six weeks before being posted to work at Plas Tirion Farm, Llanrug in October 1943 and where she worked and lived until January 1946 when she left the WLA.

"At Plas Tirion I was taught to drive by Malcolm and Jessie Mackinnon [the farmer's son and daughter]. I learnt in three weeks and then I was on my own. During the war one didn't have to pass a driving test ... I was taught to drive so that I could deliver milk in the Ford van to Llanrug, Cwm-y-Glo, and Llanberis. (I was) called at 6am to milk. Then I would go in for breakfast and change into clean overalls and start on the milk round. No bottles, the milk had to be measured so I carried a pint, half pint and a quarter pint measure..."

For some girls used to a warm and comfortable office or shop, the transformation to working with the WLA often in cold and wet conditions, proved to be too much. But many became very capable and took on the challenge of every type of job including the destruction of pigeons, sparrows, rabbits, squirrels and rats, considered to be pests because of the vast quantity of human food that they consumed.

The Women's Timber Corps, formed in 1942, undertook the task of tree felling with the aid of axes, which could weigh up to 7lbs, and cross saws. Many of the trees planted on a hill a few miles from Llanberis to commemorate the Jubilee of Queen Victoria, were cut down to be used as telegraph poles and pit props depending on their dimensions. [NLW Ms 23073D] After felling, the trees were dragged by horses, with the aid of chains, to a suitable clearing. It was here that Mrs Megan Edwards from Llansadwrn and othermembers of the team went to work on the trees, cutting or trimming as the case may be. She recalls that the area where they worked was also used for bomb storage and entry could only be gained by the production of a special pass to the police. Similar work was carried out at the plantation on the other side of the road to the *Royal Victoria Hotel*.

Mrs Ida Houston, another member of the indomitable team, recalls her time working in the woods:

"... in the winter, when it was snowing, we used to have a bonfire and burn all the odd twigs and bits of wood. This was fun and we used to roast potatoes on the embers. A little finch used to come by. He had only one leg and we called him 'Hoppity'. Naturally we gave him crumbs..."

When bad weather brought work to a halt, Mrs Mary Jones from Speke, Liverpool recalls that cover was sought in the RAF

dispelled resulting in 19,000 being employed by the harvest of 1941. A report in a local paper stated that only a few had joined the WLA in Caernarvonshire by September 1939 and an appeal was launched for more volunteers. [C&DH 15.9.39] Its members were recruited from shops, offices, hair salons and even actresses came to fill the gaps created when the men went off to war but the work was more physically demanding than that which they had encountered in civilian life.

Each girl was guaranteed employment for twelve months with one week's holiday with pay and, unless there was urgent seasonal work to be tackled, the girls were usually allowed to be off duty on Saturday and Sunday afternoons. No deductions were made owing to sickness, injury or wet weather stoppage. Those under 18 years of age were paid a wage of 18/- (90p) per week together with their keep and those over 18 received £1.2s.6d (£1.12 ¹/₂p) per week (by 1944 this had been increased to £2.8s per week) plus keep. This wage was sometimes enhanced when 9¹/₂d overtime was paid on weekdays. The uniform with which they were provided consisted of a pair of brown corduroy breeches, a beige shirt, a green jumper, a khaki overcoat, a brown hat, a thick pair of stockings, wellington boots, a pair of heavy brown shoes and 2 pairs of boots. [GAS

underground air raid shelters, until such time as the foresters built a wooden hut for them where they were able to enjoy a cup of tea and obtain warmth from a wood-burning stove. On such occasions, the peace and solitude of the forest were often disturbed by raucous singing emanating from within the hut.

The winter weather brought many problems in the Snowdonia hills including that of transport.

The girls were paid £2 per week from which those who were in digs had to pay £1.2.6 which left little pocket money. At that time, every penny mattered and for that reason if they went to the cinema it would be to Llanberis or Caernarvon at a cost of six pence, the same as the forces, whereas civilian or non-uniform rates applied in the Plaza and City Cinemas in Bangor. Also at Caernarvon they were able to have a similar concession at the YMCA paying 2d for a cup of tea and cake. The same cost of admission applied at the weekly dance held at the *Royal Victoria Hotel*, Llanberis and the twice weekly dance at the village hall.

To save on capital outlay and, in particular, to ensure that farm machinery would be fully used, it was the policy of the War Agricultural Executive Committee through its Machinery Department to hire its various implements wherever required at a cost to the farmer of £5 per week. Requests for assistance from farmers to a central control would result in the appropriate machine and driver being allocated for the task. A similar hire arrangement existed with contractors who used their own drivers. The WAEC preferred the hiring arrangement because the machinery would be better utilised at a time when there was a severe shortage and an increasing workload.

The severe winter of 1939-40 brought many problems and the cessation of nearly all work on the land at a time when much required to be done. When the Spring came, it brought with it floods from melting snow and mud that clung to everything including farming implements and footwear. Nevertheless, throughout the UK 2,000,000 new acres had been ploughed and were ready for sowing by the Spring.

The drivers operated on a shift basis but tractors and implements carried on regardless of weather or time. There would be no respite for the drivers during severe winter weather; the only concession allowed was a folded sack placed on the cold wet metal seat in an attempt to ease the discomfort. When pressure of work demanded or when a hired tractor was required on another site, work would continue at night by moonlight or with screened headlights and a lamp placed in the hedge to act as guide for the driver. Although an extra hour had been added to the normal British Summer Time during the war, there was a tendency for some farmers in the remoter parts of the country to ignore the 'official' time as they had no desire to upset the sole timepiece of the household!

As more land became available for cultivation so the demand on the labour force grew due, in the main, to the improved harvests. On these occasions, children, evacuees, shop girls and office workers were brought on to the land to gather in the crops. Camps, hostels, village halls and schools were provided to cope with this vast army of temporary workers and this is where they slept and ate. Many preferred to spend their holidays working on the land and so help the war effort. 12,000 youngsters, accommodated in 300 camps, assisted with the 1941 harvest including those belonging to the Liverpool Boys Institute who were paid 8d an hour when they went to work at the Schoolboy Harvest Camp at Plas Newydd. (UCNW PNP 5723)

The Federation of Young Farmers' Clubs, formed in 1942, arranged for Ministry of Information films to be shown and talks to be given by a WAEC Technical Officer such as Mr Ivor Wyn Jones who would advise them about the latest technology and farming methods (UCNW PNP 5723). The rally held at Plas Newydd, Llanfairpwll on Anglesey on 10 June 1944 allowed the latest farm machinery (including a 'robot transplanter') to be shown as well as various competitions between clubs to demonstrate skills at machine and hand shearing of sheep, milking competition, rope making, weight judging, potato peeling, thatch making and welding. [UCNW PNW 5719] Similar rallies were held at the Oval football ground at Caernarvon.

There was at least one farm on the outskirts of Caernarvon which had the benefit of a Titan tractor, a legacy of the First World War. Early tractor wheels were of steel with the rear ones having the benefit of lugs along the edge to give additional traction whilst the front wheels had a rim running along the centre to give better steerage. These vintage machines were started by means of petrol prior to switching over to Tractor Vaporising Oil (TVO). Many of these early tractors could only tow certain implements but the Ferguson TE20 (known as the 'Little Grey Fergie' or *'Ffergi Bach'*) developed in 1945 had the benefit of a 'three point link system'. This allowed the driver, through the hydraulic system on the tractor, to make adjustments, such as the depth of a furrow when ploughing, without dismounting from the vehicle. Fifty years on, these reliable and popular tractors which revolutionised farming, are still in use long after production ceased.

In Wales, the tractor with caterpillar tracks was considered to be a very versatile vehicle because it could tackle the most difficult hillside terrain where a plough had never ventured before. These powerful machines, turning over four or five furrows at a time, could do the work of many horses and men but until tractors became available generally, horses continued to be actively engaged on Welsh farms and were traded on a regular basis as the following report shows (a team of horses could rarely accomplish more than half an acre per day whereas modern tractors can now accomplish around twenty acres in a similar period):

"... Menai Bridge Horse Fair - John Pritchard & Co. conducted ...their two day sale ... on Tuesday when 270 seasoned horses, three year old, light horses, Welsh cobs and ponies (were sold). A further 400 were sold on Wednesday ..." [C&DH 27.10.39]

1940 saw the first Sunshine binders coming from Kilkenny in Australia as well as Massey Harris from Canada and International from the USA. They would arrive mostly assembled and ready for use, the exception being the binder with its fans and blades packed separately. They would be delivered by rail to Llangefni or Caernarvon or were collected by lorry from a distribution centre at Cambridge especially when there was a shortage of railway wagons as was often the case during the war.

In the 1940s a pick-up baler cost about £299 and a tractor about the same price. Even when second-hand farming implements were offered for sale permission had to be obtained from the WAEC before the transaction could be completed. The WAEC had 884 machines in use on Anglesey farms, including 77 tractors by February 1944 but by 1953 this number had risen to 1,273. At the same time there were 1,651 tractors in use in Caernarvonshire (the WAEC continued to control farming methods for some years after the war).

It was the custom in Anglesey for farm workers to present themselves for employment for a period of six months at a bi-annual fair (*ffair cyflogi*) held at Llangefni in May and October. The improvement in agricultural wages by increasing the minimum wage by 8s. to 48s added £14.9 million to farming costs. Further increases occurred in December 1943 when the minimum wage went up to 65s and 70s in March 1945. Agricultural workers were sometimes provided with food and, in the case of the single men, accommodation at the place of work. Unfortunately, wage increases could not always be absorbed because of insufficient income and this resulted in a tendency for the farmer to rely more and more on employing casual rather than regular labour and by contracting the War Agricultural Committee to carry out the work on his behalf with their own workers.

At the same time as the land was being improved so too was the quality of stock although the elimination of tuberculosis from cows was not completed until after the war. The Milk Officer employed by the WAEC carried out a periodic check on the quantity and quality of milk and if it was found that insufficient was being produced or that it was not up to the required standard then the farmer or milk retailer was liable to lose his licence and the right to sell milk.

Mr Evan Hughes of Ty Mawr, Pontllyfni milked by hand until around 1943 but in the following years, by making use of the nearby Afon Llifon which powered a Pelton wheel, sufficient electricity was generated to supply lighting in the house and the use of some small appliances as well as a milking machine. The milk which he produced to retail amongst his customers at around 3d a pint was taken daily from house to house, within a radius of five miles from the farm, with the aid of a horse drawn milk float.

Any surplus milk was sold to the Milk Marketing Board (MMB), which had been started before the war, and taken by rail from Chwilog to Liverpool. Compared to present day methods of milk collection from cooled bulk tanks at the farm, for many years the milk was taken in ten gallon churns by tractor from the farm to the nearest road where it was placed on a purpose built shelf on top of a hedge or wall accessible to the MMB lorry for collection twice a day. Some of the smaller farms also churned their own butter which could be for home use, for selling or to be exchanged at a local shop for other provisions. A wooden stamp applied to the half pound of butter to give an impression of an animal or object would be the means of identifying the source.

In preference to purchasing meats from a local butcher, it was possible for a farmer to apply for a Ministry of Food permit for one of his own pigs or lambs to be taken to a local slaughter-house such as Isaac Parry's at the Victoria Dock at Caernarvon. The meat was then preserved by covering in saltpetre prior to being wrapped in muslin or by soaking in a slate tank filled with brine where it would remain for three or four weeks. The farmer's ration book would be adjusted in accordance with the weight of the animal slaughtered. Preserved hams or joints of meat hanging from the farmhouse ceiling were quite a familiar sight and in this state they could be kept for about six months. To overcome the lack of refrigeration which presented as much of a problem to the retailing butcher as it did to the householder, a lamb or pig would be purchased from a nearby farm and slaughtered the following day so providing his customers with fresh meat.

Each year of the war saw an improvement in the state of British farms with new land brought into production where nothing of use grew before. Between 1939 and 1944 6,500,000 additional acres were brought under the plough in the UK and, because of a six-fold use in the application of lime and fertiliser, there was a tremendous improvement in the land and subsequent yield. In the case of animals there was an increase of 300,000 in milking cows and other cattle increased by 400,000 whereas there was a decrease in sheep by 6,300,000, pigs by 2,500,000 and poultry by 19,200,000 in the same period.

From an atmosphere of neglect the countryside had assumed an air of a thriving industry. Agricultural wages had improved and the former disparity with other industrial wages had to a certain extent been removed. A vast increase in mechanisation had taken place both to assist in increasing production and to ease the difficulties which had arisen from the loss of men to the Armed Forces and other industries.

Rationing

Plans for the rationing of food had been formulated in 1936 by the Food (Defence) Plans Department of the Board of Trade so that by the outbreak of war, the machinery of control both in respect of commodities and local organisation was largely ready. The Minister of Food and his staff were evacuated to North Wales and the country's food rationing system, which began in January 1940, was operated from various commandeered hotels in Colwyn Bay by 5,000 clerks. The Divisional Food Offices, in addition to their supervisory function, were responsible for providing accommodation for emergency food stocks known as "Buffer Depots" for supporting normal distribution services. A number of buildings were requisitioned for temporary storage, including the Pavilion at Caernarvon, until new buildings were erected. [GAS 1301/24]

There were three regional offices of the Ministry of Food in Caernarvon with the Bangor Street office under Major Lloyd Griffith responsible for the whole of North Wales. A separate office in the same street, under the charge of Mr Quinn (who had been with J Bibby and Sons, Liverpool) dealt with the allocation and distribution of oils and fats to wholesaler users such as bakeries, cafés and ice cream makers. The third office at Pool Side dealt with the distribution of ration books.

Food Rationing began on 8 January 1940 with a weekly allowance per person of: 4 ozs bacon or ham, 4ozs butter, 12ozs sugar. Within six months the weekly allowance was reduced to 2ozs of tea, 2ozs cooking fat, 4ozs margarine, 2ozs of butter (later to be further reduced to 1oz). Meat was rationed from 11 March 1940 with a weekly allowance of l/10d (9p) rather than by weight which enabled people to choose the type and quality they preferred. Within the next twelve months, further rationing of jams, marmalade, honey etc., followed by cheese was also introduced.

Other foodstuffs such as poultry, game, fish and bread were restricted by availability. Every opportunity would be taken to acquire eggs and these would be preserved in water glass, a chemical which sealed the shell. Many substitutes came on the market such as dried powdered egg and powdered milk but they were not very popular nor was coffee substitute which was made from ground dried acorns. Because icing was banned, tiered wedding cakes were often made of cardboard and hired from bakers.

The National Wholemeal Loaf was of a bran-like texture and was an unpopular substitute for white bread. Many decided to use their back gardens to keep pigs and hens so as to supplement their rations and to use any household food waste for feeding.

Although many items of food were rationed it did not follow that they were always available; some went 'under the counter' and were sold at the discretion of the shopkeeper. This discriminatory distribution caused some animosity especially after housewives had queued patiently and then discovered that the items required were not available. Shopkeepers would generally try and look after people who had been regular customers before the war.

As the result of the *Dig for Victory* campaign, members of the Women's Institute arranged for collected fruit to be preserved or made into jam. The WI also had the task of co-ordinating the

German Prisoners of War at Vaynol POW Camp, Bangor, shortly after the war.
[Mr Ludger Lonnemann]

Ty Mawr, Pontllyfni.
L-R: Mr William Hughes, Mrs Jane Hughes, Feru Emilio (Italian PoW), Arthur Roberts.
[Mr Evan D Hughes]

Aliens Pass issued to German Prisoner of War Richard Stuhlfelder. These were issued to POWs who were working on farms after the war.
[Mr Richard Stuhlfelder]

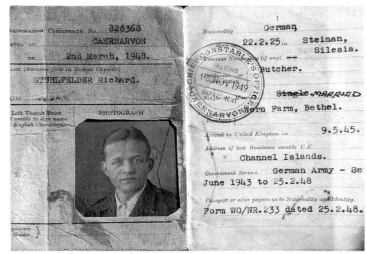

collection and distribution of vegetables and fruit produced in thousands of allotments and gardens, also the collection of rose hips by children, which, in syrup form, supplied beneficial vitamins.

In order that the basic food level could be maintained in the UK at a time when British shipping was suffering heavy losses from U-boat action, the British Food Mission in Washington liaised with the American authorities under the Lend Lease Act 1941 for supplies of food to be shipped for the civilian population and armed forces.

"No weapon ever invented is more deadly than hunger; it can spike guns, destroy courage, and break the will of the most resolute peoples. The finest armies in the world, courageous enough in the face of bombs or bullets, can be reduced by it to helplessness and surrender...'
[*Land at War 1939-44* HMSO 1945]

The Ministry of Food published recipes in daily newspapers in an effort to help housewives concoct palatable meals for their families. Many of these recipes were based on the potato which housewives were urged to use when baking in preference to imported flour. Wartime summer cookery classes were run in 1943 by the Caernarvonshire Education Committee for anyone who cared to enrol. [GAS XD 39/240]

Clothes, material and shoes were rationed from 1 June 1941 when everyone was issued with a clothing book. Standardisation of clothing produced 'Utility' garments which, although well made with good material by well known firms, were nevertheless devoid of style or character. Such clothing was identified by the symbol – CC41 (Civilian Clothing 1941).

With the introduction of petrol rationing on 16 September 1939 only one grade was thereafter available and this was sold and distributed as 'pool' motor spirit at 1/6d per gallon. The normal petrol coupons were obtained from Post or Taxation Offices but applications for supplementary coupons had to be submitted to the Divisional Petroleum Office. The lack of transport and fuel often necessitated farmers moving sheep and cows on the hoof to market or from summer to winter pasture and back again in the Spring. It was not uncommon for animals to be walked a distance in excess of twenty miles as were the sheep from Dyffryn Mymbyr which went as far as Colwyn Bay where they would graze on the golf course during the winter months. Since there was always a possibility that a farmer might be stopped by the police and asked to justify his journey, there was a tendency for suitable merchandise, such as a sack of potatoes to be carried in the boot. Naturally, such a sack travelled many miles but never appeared to leave the car. In an attempt to overcome the problem of petrol shortage, the Crosville bus company converted 10% of their fleet to run on coal or producer gas which reduced the speed of the vehicles to 15-18 mph.

Rationing of electricity, coal and gas supplies was introduced on 8 September 1939 when attempts were made to regulate the quantity being used. However, because of administrative problems it was abandoned after a fortnight and no further attempts were made to control sales or usage. Thereafter, as with some foodstuffs, it was a question of availability.

Prisoners of War

From 1943, many Prisoners of War (PoW), both Italian and German, were allocated for agricultural duties and for such assistance the farmer had to pay the WAEC between £2.10 and £3 per week. [UCNW PNP 5724] The work carried out by these prisoners was very much appreciated by farmers especially at a time when they were desperately short of labour and the potatoes needed harvesting. The German prisoner, considered to be a more diligent worker when compared to other continental nationalities, worked well alongside regular farm workers and members of the Women's Land Army. They were popular because they were willing and capable of tackling most jobs on the farm although, generally, they had not experienced such work in civilian life.

After the experience of staying in PoW camps in England, such as Oswestry and Sheffield, they gladly accepted the opportunity of agricultural work in preference to incarceration within barbed wire when they realised that the British had no intention of releasing them in the near future even after hostilities ceased in 1945.

Some of the groups destined for Gwynedd were very surprised at the hostile reception awaiting them in the form of farmers armed with pitchforks! Prior to their arrival, none of the prisoners knew anything about Wales so it came as a surprise to them that the people spoke a different language. Having learnt some English since coming into the country, they now found that they had to start all over again!

The first PoWs into the area were Italians who were housed in Gwynedd camps such as Pontllyfni and Bontnewydd, both on the outskirts of Caernarvon; Vaynol near Bangor; Sarn, Nefyn and Four Crosses near Pwllheli and these were controlled from the headquarters at Pabo Hall, Llandudno Junction. Conditions in the camp were generally quite good with plenty of reading material provided and studying encouraged. When the Italians were replaced by the German prisoners the same facilities were provided together with German newspapers printed in London and newsletters printed in Ruthin. As part of their recreation they would play football against RAF personnel from Llandwrog.

During the period when the army was responsible for the prisoners, the men were taken by lorry to whichever farm they had been allocated and in an attempt to prevent familiarity between prisoners and farmers, the venue was changed each week. The following instruction was issued by the military authorities:

"PoW labour (described as Italian cooperators) not to leave employer's land during the working day. Do not go to any villages or towns or any shops, houses, hotels or restaurant. Do not receive money or gifts. Do not send letters except through the hutment hostel to which they are attached. Food will be provided with normal rations including a haversack lunch by the Military Authorities. It will not be necessary for the employer to provide cooperators with food but only with hot liquid refreshments (eg cocoa, coffee or soup) during the day..."

However, when, at the end of the war, the WAEC took responsibility from the army for the distribution of labour and allocation of work, a different attitude prevailed to the extent that it was not unusual for farmers to telephone the camp and indicate which prisoner they would prefer to work for them. The method of transport was also changed with prisoners being allocated bicycles for getting to work.

Work started at 8am and finished at 5pm with a lunch break in between when the prisoners partook of food supplied by the camp. In practice however, because they were always hungry this would have been consumed long before the official break and they invariably joined the family to share their meal at midday. Such was the compatibility between prisoner and their 'employer' that within a short space of time they were treated as a member of the family and allowed to stay at the farm rather than at the PoW camp. Heinz Nowack was one such person and when he was released from his Prisoner of War status and granted his Aliens Certificate in January 1948, he continued working at Ty Mawr, Pontllyfni and later at Yoke House, Pwllheli, with the same family in preference to returning to Germany. His wage, however, has improved somewhat from the derisory 1d per hour which he was receiving as a PoW in 1946!

The German prisoners destined to stay at the camp (later to

Mr David Lloyd George, MP (centre) with Dame Margaret Lloyd George (right of centre) and Mr Percy Hunting (left of centre) during the negotiations for the establishment of the NECACO factory at Llanberis.
[Hunting Plc]

DINORWIC SLATE QUARRIES, LLANBERIS.   214105

The Dinorwic Quarry. The white buildings beside the lake were occupied by NECACO during the war.
[Miss Iris Morley Jones]

NECACO Staff
[Dewi Ellis]

The front fuselage sections of Avro Lancaster bombers being assembled at the NECACO factory, Llanberis. [Hunting Plc]

become the forestry yard) on the Vaynol estate outside Bangor, were taken by train in August 1945 to Menai Bridge station from where they were marched, a distance of some two miles, to accommodation which they found to consist of tents previously occupied by Italian PoWs. Eventually three Nissen huts were delivered and erected by them to house twenty prisoners in each. The camp, which was located near to the Capel Graig Lodge, was guarded by five British soldiers but they were regarded as superfluous since none of the prisoners had any desire to escape. Amongst the prisoners who came to Vaynol was Ludger Lonnemann, who had been conscripted into the Wehrmacht. After serving in Poland and Russia as a paratrooper in the 2nd Parachute Division he was posted to France where he was captured near Brest by the American army in September 1944. Richard Stuhlfelder was conscripted at the age of 17 into the German airborne forces in 1942. It was however, as an infantryman that he fought in Normandy following the Allied landings of 1944. After being wounded in both knees at St Malo he was taken by German hospital ship to Guernsey. At the end of the war, he was taken to Oswestry before being transferred to Vaynol.

Although they were issued with a uniform POWs tended to make their own clothes; a bed sheet would make a reasonable shirt or two whilst ties were made out of curtain material and shoes out of a pair of boots. Indeed they were adept at making most things to the extent that 'ships in bottles' or even in electric light bulbs would be manufactured in sufficient quantity that they were able to sell them to Caernarvon shops. Letter openers made out of old tooth brushes were also a saleable item in times of austerity which followed the war years.

The emergency food supply kept during the war at the Pavilion at Caernarvon was used to feed the prisoners and this together with fresh bread, butter, corned beef, or boiled ham was distributed round the camps twice a week by lorry. Clothing and footwear were replaced when necessary.

CHAPTER 10: Industry

Manufacturing – Aircraft Industry – NECACO

Rollason Aircraft Services, formed by Bill Rollason and Freddie Kent in 1935, had its workshops conveniently located on Croydon airfield enabling it to service aeroplanes for British Continental Airways, Imperial Airways, Vickers and Hawker Aircraft. It also had contracts with the Air Ministry to repair and recondition service aircraft such as the Fairey Battle and Hawker Hurricane. Components for the Wellington bomber aircraft were also being manufactured on behalf of Vickers. Within four years, Hunting and Son Ltd., had become the majority shareholder of Rollason and the Chairman, Mr Percy Hunting, had joined the board. When extra work was imposed on the company by the Ministry of Aircraft Production at the outbreak of war, additional industrial capacity was found at Hanworth, Ruislip and Tollerton near Nottingham because of the limited space available at its main factory at Croydon.

A bombing attack by German aircraft at 7.10pm on Sunday 15 August 1940 resulted in Rollason's Aircraft Services' Croydon factory being extensively damaged and six workers losing their lives. Aircraft, both inside the factory and outside on the runway, were damaged or destroyed. Further damage was inflicted when the raiders returned the following night. Although production continued in temporary premises, it became obvious that safer quarters would have to be found.

Mr Percy Hunting accompanied by a couple of officials from the factory, travelled by train to Caernarvon on Tuesday 27 August 1940 where they were met by the Mayor, Mr Philip Davies the town clerk and his wife, the Rt. Hon. David Lloyd George MP and Major Goronwy Owen MP. The next day, after breakfast at the *Royal Hotel*, Mr Percy Hunting, together with Mr Lloyd George and Major Owen, had a look at a couple of quarries. After lunch with Sir Michael Assheton Smith, Mr Vivian (the Vaynol Agent) and Mr O T Williams

NECACO Inspection Staff, Llanberis.
[Mrs Iris Morley Jones]

NECACO Staff Drama Group.
[Mrs Iris Hughes]

NECACO Staff.
[Mr Dewi Ellis]

NECACO Works Pass issued to Mr Haydn Hughes.
Note the reference to the designated
air raid shelter bottom right.
[Mr Haydn Hughes]

(the General Manager), Mr Hunting had further discussion with Mr Lloyd George and his family at Criccieth over tea. On Friday 30 August, the decision was made to go ahead with the Llanberis project.

The North East Coast Aircraft Company (NECACO) had been formed before the war in Newcastle-upon-Tyne as a subsidiary of Hunting and Company. When the decision was made to re-locate the factory, the ready-made company, which had never become involved in the original intention of manufacturing aircraft because of possible danger from air attacks in the north-east, took over the new enterprise at Llanberis and operated under the acronym of NECACO. Although it later changed its name to Hunting Aviation, it continued to be known by its old name of NECACO.

According to a letter dated 16 September 1940 sent by Mr O T Williams to the quarry solicitors, it seemed that he was anything but pleased with losing the shed facilities:

"... the government have demanded the taking over on behalf of Rollason Aircraft Services Ltd. certain sheds and other small buildings

from the Dinorwic Quarry...at a rental of £1,200 plus £20 for the use of the tunnel ..."

Possible problems may have been anticipated with such a take-over when a letter stated:

"... (NECACO) carrying on a very big aircraft production industry under Government orders ... also appreciate that slates are now of considerable national importance and that the two industries must try and work smoothly together ..." [letter 28.4.41]

On 6 May 1941, Rollason stated:

"I am afraid that in this part of Wales they have had such a peaceful time that they have not realised the importance of this aircraft manufacture ..."

The use of 'the tunnel' (originally planned as an Air Raid Shelter according to some of the letters passing between the Dinorwic Quarry manager and solicitors) was a permanently contentious issue with accusations that NECACO were trespassing on to the part allocated for use by the quarry – even though the quarry manager had been told by their own solicitors that NECACO were acting within the rights bestowed by war-time requisition laws.

Mr Arthur Summers, who had joined the company in 1940 to take charge of the relocation, had the responsibility in the first place of preparing one shed, 561 feet long, previously used to house some one hundred and fifty machines used in splitting and cutting slate, for equipment which was brought by road from Croydon. Engineers such as Mr Bill Lavender and Mr Fred Lane planned the layout of the machines and, later, Fred Lane took charge of the training of personnel in a building originally owned by the Caernarvon Electric Company on the Bangor side of Victoria Dock at Caernarvon. Another shed 184 feet long was also acquired and used by NECACO. Summers, together with a small band of employees from Croydon, completed the task by the end of September enabling the production of some components and aircraft parts to start by November and reach full production by Spring 1941.

During the time when Percy Hunting looked after matters in North Wales he lived at Llywenarth, Penygroes, the home of Col. Jones-Roberts, with the resident house-keeper taking care of the place.

If unemployment had been a problem in the 1930s it was certainly not so during the Second World War. On the contrary, with the exodus of men and women to the armed forces and other destinations, the task of finding sufficient people to work in munitions and similar occupations, was a daunting one. The role of the Unemployment Office was changed from finding work for people to that of finding people for work. Even men who were unsuitable for military service because of ill health or age, could still be considered for work in munitions. Women, who were within a certain age category and in suitable health, were usually given the option of either enrolling in the armed forces or being directed into work of national importance, such as munitions.

When NECACO started in Llanberis, the company had the difficult task of training some three thousand people, many of whom had never even seen the inside of a factory let alone operated machinery. Limited training was given at the Victory Works on Victoria Dock in Caernarvon in operating machines but most

apprentices became proficient within a short space of time by practical experience in Llanberis. [GAS XC12/1/87]

Women who had previously been involved with housework and caring for husbands and children, were suddenly transformed into experts in the assembly of intricate pieces of metal so as to form a vital part of an aircraft. The secretarial staff were interviewed at the *Royal Hotel*, Caernarvon and the initial office for their use was set up there until such time as facilities were available at Llanberis. Tea or coffee was brought to them on a silver salver by Sir Michael Duff's valet who had been directed there for war-time work. In time, Mr Summers the General Manager, Mr Cowan the Assistant Manager and Mr Young the works manager moved into an office made up of two huts near the main shed at Llanberis but, because it was so basic, use was made of toilet facilities at the *Padarn Villa Hotel*. Eventually they joined the accountants Mr Sanderson, Mr Bowran and Mr Tongue in the main shed which by then housed all the clerical staff.

The first jigs to be installed at Llanberis were for producing Defiant night fighter wings. When it was fully operational, the factory produced parts for the Halifax, Lancaster, Stirling and Wellington bombers. It also undertook occasional work for Saunders Roe at Beaumaris. In addition to the main factory at Llanberis, there were three sites at Caernarvon involved with the manufacture or assembly of various parts: Central Garage for the Mosquito and Beaufort aircraft; a factory built on the site of the old Peblig brickworks for the outer casing for Gloster Meteor jet engines and Victory Works, on the side of the Victoria Dock, for training and producing small parts used in the main factory at Llanberis. Rivet annealing was also carried out there when the plant at Llanberis either broke down or could not cope with demand.

The tooling machines, with their pervading smell of oil, had initially been installed in the main shed, but they were later moved to the safety of a nearby tunnel (which was the subject of so much controversy with the Dinorwic Quarry manager) which ran from the site occupied by NECACO, through to Gilfach Ddu. Zinc sheets lined the roof to prevent water, which seeped out of the rock above, falling on to the capstans, lathes, planers and grinders and respective

Aerial view of the Saunders Roe works at Beaumaris.
[Mr W Williams]

Staff at the Saunders Roe works, Beaumaris.
[Mr John Morris]

Launching a Catalina flying boat at
Saunders Roe, Beaumaris.
[Mr W Williams]

A Mariner flying boat on the lawn in front of 'Fryars',
Beaumaris.
[Mr W Williams]

A Kingfisher at Beaumaris. [Mr W Williams]

Motor Torpedo Boat T201, built at Saunders Roe, Beaumaris.
Work on aircraft ceased at Beaumaris in September 1945
and the factory was then involved in the design and manufacture
of such diverse items as MTBs, mine sweepers and lifeboats.
[Mr John Morris]

Coronado at Beaumaris. [Mr John Morris]

Saunders Roe staff at 'Fryars', Beaumaris
[Mr John Morris]

operators. Even so, the atmosphere was dank and damp. The various machines were located on one side of the tunnel which barely allowed a small low-loader Lister pick-up with its engine mounted on the front steering wheel, to travel inside. An hydraulic press for rubber parts was installed at Gilfach Ddu and the quarry pattern shop was also used for certain items. A Rushton engine, brought from Preston, powered a generator to provide emergency power if the national electricity supply had failed for any reason.

Since there was always the possibility of an air attack, teams of personnel from each of the factories visited RAF Llandwrog periodically for instructions from Sgt. W A Wilson (RAF Fire Instructor) in the art of fire-fighting and extinguishing incendiary bombs with stirrup pumps. As part of the training he would also let them have the experience of walking through fire in asbestos suits. If an air raid warning sounded the personnel took refuge within the machine tunnel.

There were two shifts of twelve hours each from 7.30 am to 7.30 pm and 7.30pm to 7.30 am at NECACO with people working a day shift for two weeks followed by two weeks of night work. The latter shift was much quieter compared to the day shift as there were fewer people working. Unless there was pressure for certain parts, work usually finished at 4pm on Saturday and resumed when the Sunday morning shift came in. When the workload began to ease because of greater expertise and organisation, production staff were allowed to finish at 5pm on Wednesdays and midday on Saturdays.

Crosville buses, both single and double decker, some starting from Beaumaris at 6.10 am, would tour the countryside picking up men and women until the well laden vehicle, with its contingent of songsters, arrived at Llanberis at 7.15 am in time for the start of the shift. Similar arrangements applied to the workers at the Peblig, Central Garage and Victory works at Caernarvon.

During the day shift, a fifteen minute tea break was allowed in the morning and afternoon together with an hour's break for lunch, which, in the summer time, was often taken by the side of the lake. Similar concessions were allowed on the night shift. During the winter months when employees worked the day shift and consequently saw little if any daylight, they were given the opportunity of sun-ray lamp (ultra violet) treatment at the medical centre. Provisions for the canteen were replenished periodically by sending one of the drivers to the Pavilion at Caernarvon where butter, tea and sugar were stored for general and emergency use.

Wages varied, with the basic pay supplemented by piece work or bonus, depending on the output. Girls at the factory received 1/- an hour but if special training had been received then the rate was increased to 1/3d per hour with 11d bonus as compared to a man who received 2/6d per hour. The clerical staff were also subjected to long hours of hard work resulting in a strong desire for nothing more than sleep after a hasty meal when home was reached at the end of a shift. If anyone complained because of long hours, they were reminded that members of the armed forces, fighting on their behalf, never complained. At the end of a shift, irrespective of how tired they were, enough strength was mustered to run the distance between the shed and the buses so as to grab a seat rather than have to stand. The period at home was short, but long enough for a meal and a sleep which would enable them to recuperate sufficiently for the next shift.

Problems with the workforce were not unknown from time to time but more often than not disputes were quickly settled. However, one strike at Llanberis was caused by one of the girls taking more time than she should for 'powdering her nose'. A confrontation with a foreman and the involvement of a union official caused the factory to be brought out on strike which lasted for a couple of days.

Until purpose-built lorries were available, vehicles would be commandeered from local firms for carrying both the raw materials and the finished products. By the time production at Llanberis had reached its zenith, fourteen 'Queen Mary' lorries were being used to carry parts manufactured at Llanberis and Caernarvon. These vehicles always carried two drivers to deal with any problems encountered on their journey, and to ensure that no one driver exceeded his permitted maximum eleven hours duty. A delivery to Weybridge, south west of London, entailed leaving Llanberis at 4pm and arriving some time after 10am the following morning. Parts were also delivered from Llanberis to the Fairey Aviation factory at Alston, Cumbria. The lorries seldom, if ever, returned empty from the south since material was usually brought from Gloucester for use at Llanberis.

The twelve hour shift at the factory left workers feeling very tired with little incentive to enjoy the facilities provided at the NECACO works club at Gronant, Pool Side, Caernarvon. Nevertheless, the dances held there, especially on Saturday nights, were enjoyed by most employees. Members of the band who played for the dances were Mr J L Jones on drums (he was responsible for designing the Horn with Wings logo of the company) together with Mr Geoff Roberts on piano, Mr Bill Collins on violin and Mr Haydn Hughes the popular vocalist. In another room Mr J L Jones' wife ran a lending library and snooker tables were available on the ground floor. A drama group was formed with Mrs Iris Hughes, Mr Lionel Hughes, Mr Arthur Hutchinson, Miss Kathleen Mason, Mrs Olive Roe, Mrs Betty Williams, to name but a few of the local talent, to perform plays such as Agatha Christie's *Alibi* and these were presented to packed houses at the Guildhall at Caernarvon.

Concerts held at Gronant when local personalities were given an opportunity of displaying their talents, were always very popular. Indeed, the standard at such concerts was considered by many to be far higher than the entertainment provided by ENSA (Entertainment National Service Association) concert parties when they performed at the works canteen from time to time. The popular NECACO male voice and mixed voice choirs with Mr Aled Owen as choir master, practised at the Gronant club and entertained many in the district as well as competing at the National Eisteddfod at Llandudno. Mr David Lloyd, a well known tenor at that time, used to sing to an appreciative audience at the Peblig canteen. The BBC radio programme *Workers' Playtime* which was broadcast from various factories around the country also visited NECACO at Llanberis but, because of the condition of the canteen piano, the BBC brought their own instrument.

The alternative to the present day transistor radio at the inspection hut was a gramophone on which endless records would be played with a scratchy sound emanating from a large horn speaker. Although cumbersome, the equipment would be taken outside during the summer months for a dance and the sound of Glen Miller's *String of Pearls* and *Moonlight Serenade* would be heard drifting over Llyn Peris. For further relaxation members of the staff ran a tennis club at the *Padarn Villa Hotel* with matches played against members of the BBC Variety Club at Bangor and RAF personnel from 31 MU Llanberis.

Paradoxically, many officials and visitors called from time to time at NECACO but, because of the dearth of suitable accommodation (most of the local hotels had been taken over by the armed forces) in this relatively remote area, Hunting Aviation formed a company called Red Dragon Hotels Ltd. for the purchase of the *Padarn Lake Hotel* (later to be renamed *Padarn Valley Hotel*), the *Swallow Falls Hotel* at Betws y Coed and the *Café Royal* at Colwyn Bay. Although the company was reasonably successful, Hunting Group decided that this was one line of business that it would not be pursuing in the future. The Duke of Kent, who visited the factory on 8 May 1942 stayed with Sir Michael Duff at Vaynol as did Princess Marina when she also visited Llanberis on another occasion.

Undoubtedly, NECACO was a very successful operation with everyone from machinist to clerical staff making a valuable contribution. The consensus of opinion expressed by those who worked at the factory is that, although the work was often tiring and demanding, in retrospect, the friendly atmosphere amongst the workers made the time there "the happiest days of my life".

As the result of many aircraft factories in and around Coventry being damaged by bombing, the Ministry of Aircraft Production built a factory in Bangor (after the war it was used by Darwen British Electric Motor Company and later became the Ferranti factory) and took over the city's Crosville garage on behalf of Daimler Motor Company. Radcliffe Engineering Co Ltd built a factory at Llandudno Junction in May 1940 for the manufacture of certain war materials (it was taken over by the International Refrigeration Co Ltd on 1 May 1947). [GAS XB2/417]

Saunders Roe

In September 1940, as the result of enemy action at Cowes, Isle of Wight, the seaplane manufacturer Saunders Roe decided to move its design department to the comparative safety of property which it had purchased at 'Fryars', situated a mile from Beaumaris on the east side of Anglesey. The office staff were housed in the main house whilst various sheds and hangars, some of which had been brought from Cowes, were erected in the surrounding 50 acres of land. A concrete apron extending into the nearby Menai Strait allowed amphibious aircraft to be hauled ashore.

In 1940, aircraft manufacturing companies in America and Canada were asked to carry out certain technical changes to Catalina, Kingfisher, Coronado, Seamew and Mariner aircraft so as to conform with RAF requirements but, because of delays in delivery, this arrangement was changed in favour of carrying out alterations in this country. Saunders Roe was able to exploit its flying boat expertise when it was awarded a contract by the Ministry of Aircraft Production to carry out these alterations. Production planning with regard to the number or type of aircraft due to arrive was extremely difficult if not impossible. It was even found on some occasions that alterations programmed to be carried out on planes arriving from America had been carried out during manufacture.

The first Catalina, a monoplane flying boat with retractable wing tip floats, was flown from America at the end of February 1941 to be handled by Scottish Aviation Ltd. at Greenock on the Clyde. For a number of reasons it was decided that future work would be diverted to Beaumaris, but, until the slipway was completed in April 1941 and aircraft could be hauled out of the water ashore, work on the Catalinas would be carried out while they were still on the Strait. Because of the distance between Goose Bay and Beaumaris, extra petrol tanks were installed inside the hull of the Catalina and petrol pumped to the wing tanks whilst in flight but, on arrival at Beaumaris these tanks were removed.

With the increasing amount of work it was necessary to divide the Beaumaris staff into three sections called Shetland, R.14/40 (code for the Walrus aircraft) and Catalina. Space was always at a premium and even though the 'Red Hangar' had been brought up from Cowes, it was found necessary to make use of buildings at Beaumaris, including Chesterton's garage in Chapel Street where the wooden hulls for the Walrus aircraft were constructed prior to being transported to the Isle of Wight for final assembly.

The 'Pavilion' at the end of the pier was brought into use to store loose equipment removed from aircraft on arrival whilst conversion work was carried out on the planes. Even the stables of a house called Bryn Hyfryd were utilised as the Embodiment Loan Store and equipment such as wing trestles were stored at Red Hill and Baron Hill on the outskirts of Beaumaris. By November 1943, all the stores were brought back under one roof in the West Hangar. If certain machines were unavailable at Beaumaris, NECACO (at Llanberis) carried out some work on behalf of Saunders Roe.

The number of people working at Beaumaris varied from time to time and between August and December 1941 the staff was increased from 35 to 167 and to 200 by April 1942. By July 1942 however, the number employed on the American aircraft had dropped to 100 reflecting the fact that the number of Catalina arrivals from America had fallen. By September 1942 a figure of 200 had again been reached because of the increasing numbers of Catalinas arriving in the UK. [GAS WDAG/1 & 2]

Amongst those working at Saunders Roe was Miss Winifred Brown who operated *Saro II*, a launch owned by Saunders Roe. In the 1920s she had been asked if she had thought of taking up flying as "she was good at handling cars"! After a few lessons in a Moth G-EBLV, with communication between pilot and pupil restricted to "shouting down a gas tube purchased from Woolworth", she obtained her licence on 13 April 1927. Within three years she entered for and won the Royal Aero Club King's Cup at an average speed of 102.7 mph. When she gave up flying she lived in Menai Bridge so as to be near the sea.

Once the aircraft had landed on the Strait, directions were given by

Diamond cutters and polishers, c1941.
[Mr H Wins]

Flying Control either by radio or Aldis Lamp as to mooring arrangements since the buoys extended over several miles along the Strait. If Brown was not operating *Saro II* she would use her own 45' boat named *Perula* (built at Dickie's yard Bangor and powered by a Perkins diesel engine), to guide the plane to its allotted mooring. When the plane had been secured to the buoy, Brown would take the crew ashore in the launch.

As soon as space became available ashore, the plane would be towed by the stern, so as to give more control of the direction of travel, to a point as near as possible to the slipway where it would be attached to a buoy prior to wheels or chassis being attached by a beaching party ready for hauling her up the slipway and into the factory.

Once ashore, the first task was to wash the plane down with fresh water. The guns were removed for servicing and cleaning and all removable equipment, such as clocks, emergency rations, thermos flasks etc. inside the plane were listed, checked and stored. Other checks, alterations or conversions were carried out in the 21 days or so that the aircraft was in the hangar. It was then loaded with the appropriate loose equipment before having its magnetic compass checked on the Compass Base. Once cleared for launching, Leslie Ash, the firm's test pilot and either a Saunders Roe crew or an RAF crew allotted to the firm, would take the plane for a test flight.

Extended anti-submarine patrols by the Royal Air Force Coastal

Staff of the Coventry motor manufacturer Daimler at Penrhyn Castle – the main factory was at Caernarvon Road, Bangor.
[Lady Janet Douglas Pennant & The National Trust]

Command necessitated the fitting of long range fuel tanks which enabled the Catalinas to be airborne for up to 26 hours. An early form of Radar called Anti-Submarine Vision (ASV) used in the detection of submarines was installed followed by a later development, Long Range Anti-Submarine Vision (LRASV) in the summer of 1941. The Leigh light, providing a powerful beam for detecting surface submarines during night flying operations, was also installed. The manufacturer's bomb-carrying specification was considered insufficient and this was increased from 500 lbs to 1,500 lbs allowing depth-charges to be slung underneath the plane in special racks. With a tendency for submarines to stay on the surface when attacked by planes, an extra gun was installed in the front turret or bow.

A great variety of flying boats had been seen from time to time on the Straits during the war including the Sunderland, Coronado, Mariner, Kingfisher, Seafox, Seamew and Spitfire Floatplane.

Manufacturing – Diamond Industry

The depression in trade which followed the First World War affected the diamond industry as much as any other and caused many of the highly trained workers, whose skills had been nurtured over generations in Belgium and Holland, to be laid off leaving but a handful to run depleted factories. Paradoxically, with the threat of war looming, there came a fresh demand for diamonds because of their negotiating value and transportability. Diamonds, whether gems or industrial, are prized possessions at any time, but, in time of war, their value increased considerably.

Antwerp and Amsterdam had figured prominently in the cutting and polishing of diamonds and London in the handling and selling. When war seemed inevitable a committee appointed by the British Board of Trade had the responsibility of ensuring that diamonds shipped to Antwerp and Amsterdam were stones suitable for gem cutting only. The British Government effectively placed an embargo on the export of industrial diamonds thus preventing Germany from acquiring a reserve at a time when they were so necessary for its industries.

With the invasion of Holland and Belgium by German forces, a few of the diamond cutters managed to escape to Britain but it left Germany in control of most of the labour force and diamond-cutting tools.

Owing to the vulnerability of the south coast immediately after Dunkirk, the decision was taken to establish a new diamond industry in Bangor, North Wales by transferring some of the work from Brighton.

Mr A Monnickendam, a Hatton Garden trader who was put in charge of the operation, took with him to Bangor some Dutch and Belgian diamond cutters and a few apprentices. He was also joined by Mr Henry Lek a diamond cutter and polisher who had fled with his family from Antwerp just prior to the German occupation.

The factory at Bangor was initially set up above Burton's Tailoring shop in the High Street but by the early part of 1941 it had moved to premises on the other side of the street. The polishing and cutting machines, which had been brought from Brighton, were installed and maintained by Mr Jack Davies, a local man. Small industrial diamond factories were also established in Farrar Road and near Penrhyn Hall, Bangor.

Some local boys joined the diamond workforce as apprentices straight from school and became very proficient as the result of the tuition and expertise of their continental tutors. Their wage was 15/- a week reduced to 13/6d after stoppages and they worked from 8am to 5pm. Because of its contribution to industry generally and to armaments in particular, the diamond industry was a reserved occupation and workers in the trade were not liable to be called-up into the forces.

The North Wales Chronicle for 21 March 1941 reported:
"Diamond Cutting – Bangor's New Industry – Who in Bangor prior to the war would have dared predict that the city would have become a centre of the important diamond cutting industry. But for some time a well known diamond cutting firm which had carried on business in Antwerp and Amsterdam is now operating in High Street, Bangor with a staff of sixty. In the room where they are employed on their precious stones, Dutch, English, Flemish, French and Welsh is spoken – the last language by five young local lads who have been taken on and are now learning the highly skilled trade. [GAS]

Rough diamonds were purchased from the Diamond Trading Co. and Mr Monnickendam travelled to London once a month to the diamond syndicate for an allocation of rough diamonds, such allocation being based on the size of the factory. Ninety percent of the production at Bangor was exported to the USA as part payment for armaments and other imports into the country under the Lend-Lease agreement.

The town of Colwyn Bay also became involved in the diamond trade at the beginning of the war when Mr Gerrit Wins arrived with his family from Antwerp to live at Clifton House, 9 Bay View Road. He together with Mr Max Frish formed a company, Frish and Wins Ltd. for the purpose of cutting and polishing diamonds in accommodation rented from Bevans, ironmongers in Princess Drive, Colwyn Bay. The initial consignment of diamond cutting and polishing equipment made by Slamco of New York were lost when the ship bringing them across the Atlantic was torpedoed but the second consignment arrived safely. A Dutchman by the name of Mr Biallostersky was responsible for those operating the eighteen sawing machines.

Rough diamonds, which were obtained from the Diamond Trading Company, the selling section of De Beers Consolidated Mines, were variously described as melee (from the French 'melange') which is a mixture of quality of rough diamonds, crinkled dark melee to describe irregular shaped diamonds or dark when they contain dark impurities (known as piqué in French). The size of the diamonds was established by putting them through sieves of various sizes and detailed as +12, +11 etc. When diamonds were required the purchaser would go to London and inspect 'sights' arranged every month during the war years but now held ten times a year. Payment for the diamonds was always on a cash before delivery basis.

Mr Monnickendam remained at Bangor for approximately sixteen months until November 1941 when he decided to return to Brighton accompanied by eight of the apprentices. The factory at the Liberal Club, Llys Gwynedd, Bangor was then taken over by Mr Wins and Mr Aardewerk.

At the end of the war, most of the Belgian and Dutch diamond workers returned to their respective countries and the Bangor factory was closed (although Mr M Coronel, director of Technical Diamonds Ltd. had stated that they intended to carry on their industry permanently in Bangor). Mr J K Smit, a well known manufacturer of industrial diamond tools, employed some of the workers trained by Mr Wins, when he took over the Colwyn Bay works. Mr Smit's family had left Holland before the war and had set up a factory at Coventry but, because of the intense bombing of that city, they moved to Colwyn Bay in about 1942. His uncle Mr Jan Kors was involved in bringing diamonds from the continent on HMS *Walpole* before the Germans could get hold of them and a film based on this clandestine exercise was made called *Operation Amsterdam*.

BBC Bryn Meirion, Bangor.
[UCNW Archives]

British Broadcasting Corporation

When bombing started in London the Variety Department of the British Broadcasting Corporation was first evacuated to Bristol and then, because of continuing harassment from the air, to Bangor. There had been a limited amount of sound broadcasting from Bangor since 1935 but the original studio facilities at Bryn Meirion soon proved totally inadequate with the arrival of additional artistes and technicians in October 1940.

It became necessary for the BBC to acquire additional accommodation and the Penrhyn Hall was rented from the City Council in time for the first of the *Music While You Work* series given by Billy Ternent's famous dance band. Later Bron Castell, which housed various offices and canteen, became the hub of its operations in Bangor. The County Theatre (one of three cinemas in Bangor) as well as the vestries of Twrgwynl, Horeb, St Paul's and Tabernacle and a part of the Free Library were also taken by the growing army of supporting staff for rehearsals and similar activities.

Welsh Half Hour programmes were broadcast for the benefit of forces in the Middle East and Africa with community contributions being made through the Outside Broadcast section from Connahs Quay, Rhyl and Llandudno. Many local artistes such as Triawd y Coleg accompanied by Miss Mamie Noel Jones on the piano were regularly heard on the radio as was the Welsh tenor Mr David Lloyd singing at the Pier Pavilion Llandudno, accompanied by Mr Harold Dobb. The local broadcasts were invariably produced by Mr Sam Jones.

The Grand Theatre in Llandudno housed the theatre organ played by Reginald Forte and it was from here that programmes such as *ITMA* (*It's That man Again* with Tommy Handley) *Happidrome* and *Music Hall* were broadcast initially by using a GPO landline to Bangor studios where they were recorded. One of the many comedians to participate in such programmes was Rob Wilton who would always start his act by saying "The day war broke out...".

As BBC personnel and artistes started leaving Bangor for places nearer to London in 1943, programmes such as *Happidrome* and *Music Hall* were transferred to Bangor. The two ton BBC theatre organ was also moved from Llandudno to occupy the ground floor of the County Theatre at Bangor, where it was played by Sandy

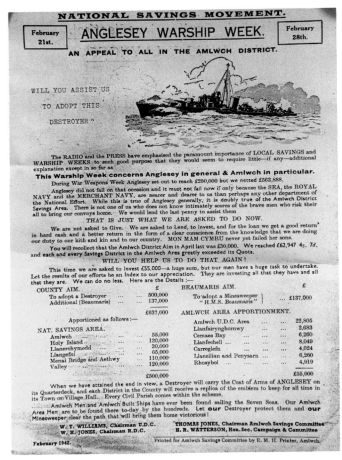

An appeal poster for National Warship Week, *1942.*
The aim was that the island of Anglesey should adopt a
destroyer and that the town of Beaumaris should adopt
the minesweeper, HMS Beaumaris.
[UCNW Archives]

Macpherson and other visiting organists. By August 1943 most of
the visitors to Bangor had returned to London.

Sadly one member of the BBC staff who had come to Bangor to
seek safety, lost his life when an enemy aircraft dropped a bomb in
the vicinity of the Maesgeirchen housing estate on the outskirts of
Bangor.

CHAPTER 11: Coastal Protection

Abermenai, considered the most vulnerable entrance to the Menai
Strait, was guarded by a flotilla of six motor patrol boats which
arrived on 6 July 1940. During the hours of darkness, they also
patrolled the coast as far south as Bardsey Island. These boats were
based at Belan Point and moorings were laid there to accommodate
them off the pier.

The Admiralty appointed Vice Admiral Hubert Lynes RN
(Retired) to be their Resident Naval Officer at the Port with the rank
of Commander and he was based at Bryn Gwyn, St David's Road,
Caernarvon. An order which he issued on 2 July 1941 stated:

"... south-western entrance to Menai Strait is closed to all Merchant
Vessels, deep sea trawlers etc. For all ports in the Menai Strait all such

vessels must enter and leave the Strait by the north-eastern entrance only
and obey the orders of the Examination Service Vessel there. The south
western entrance is open only as follows – The Men of War who for
every entry and exit will follow the procedure ordered for minor ports
with Port War Signal stations (at Fort Belan). Llanddwyn light is
temporarily extinguished and the tower and building are grey
camouflaged. All the harbour lights at Caernarvon and Port Dinorwic
are temporarily extinguished. The passage through the Strait is available
for vessels up to about 260 feet long. But even for small craft local
knowledge is essential and only very small ones should attempt the
passage except towards High Water Slacks ... Passage beneath the
Suspension Bridge or the Railway Tubular Bridge (by day or night) is
prohibited until permission has been received from the Menai Patrol
who will warn the military guard on the bridges. Failure to obtain
permission to proceed will cause the offending vessel to be fired on..."
[GAS XD15/30/95]

In a secret document headed 'Menai Bridges Broken Down' and
dated July 1941, plans were made as to the type and number of boats
required to be available for transporting people across the Strait if for
any reason either or both of the bridges became inoperative (tolls on
the Menai Bridge were abolished on 31 December 1940). In addition
to the military guard on duty on the bridges, further protection
against sabotage was provided by posting one policeman on duty
7.30am to 4pm and two from 4pm to 7.30am on the centre spans of
the Menai Suspension Bridge. [GAS XJ1234/11]

Detailed instructions concerning guarding the Menai Strait
approaches were later issued by the Resident Naval Officer,
Caernarvon which stated that there would be two flotillas, each of six
motor launches, operating from Caernarvon and Menai Bridge. The
launches were of small cruiser-yacht type painted white and armed
with a .303 machine-gun. It stated that "...t hese two Flotillas are to
reinforce, inshore, the seaward watch and guard against INVASION
which is being kept off this part of our coast...". The Caernarvon
Flotilla patrolled the area from Llanddwyn Buoy towards Bardsey
Island, while the Menai Bridge Flotilla patrolled between Great
Orme and Lynas Point. In both cases their role was to examine all
craft approaching their respective entrances and "... ensure that they
have no enemy troops, tanks, guns, or other war materials, or spies
aboard them....".

The night patrol was expected to give 'early information of the
approach of enemy invaders' and this they were expected to do with
'Firework Signals'. Three or more light rockets, which would have a
bright light lasting seven seconds in the air, would indicate an
'enemy ship or other surface craft' had been sighted. If a large
number of enemy aircraft were detected flying towards the shore
then one flash and sound rocket was to be fired. These rather vague
instructions gave no indication as to how an 'enemy ship' or 'enemy
aircraft' was to be identified especially in the dark.

The launches had no means of communication except at close
range with voice or megaphone and semaphore hand flags. It was
expected that whenever a rocket signal from the Caernarvon Flotilla
was detected by the sentry post at Coed Helen army camp, Local
Defence Volunteer Force (LDVF) (later to be renamed the Home
Guard) or the police, they were to report the matter immediately to
their respective headquarters. The Coastguard Stations and Coast
Watch Posts were expected to report any sightings to the Naval
Centre and also the Royal Naval Officer at Caernarvon.

Any signals seen emanating from the Menai Bridge Flotilla by the
LDVF on the summit of Penmaenmawr mountain or the Observer
Corps on Great Orme had to be reported to their respective
headquarters. The Menai Bridge end of the Strait was covered by the
LDVF at Red Wharf Bay, Police, Coastguard Stations and Coast

Watch Posts of the Navy.

Having been advised in September 1939 that 1,000 square yards of the timber yard at the Victoria Dock, Caernarvon had to be reserved for the "Mines Department", it came as no surprise when the Harbour Master was eventually told that the Admiralty had decided to lay a mine-field at the entrance to the Strait off Belan Point and that the mines would be of the ground type weighing 2 tons each which could be detonated from the shore. It was intended that the mine-field would be laid on 5 November 1940 at the Belan Narrows by HMS *Vernon* but the work was postponed until 3 March 1941 when HMS *Bennevis* called to ratify the area to be mined and the work was carried out on 20 March 1941 by HMS *M4*.

Similar mines, placed alongside the sea wall from a position off the Old Battery to the Oil Wharf and buried below the surface of the sea bed, could have been detonated from the shore. Additional precautions were taken with the military erecting two pill boxes – one alongside the old battery and the other abreast of the timber yard at Victoria Dock. Once the mine-field had been laid the flotilla of Patrol Boats were withdrawn. [GAS XD 15/21/4] Belan Fort was also the base for the RAF Air Sea Rescue boats and location of naval guns as additional precaution against unauthorised entry into the Menai Strait.

Drifting mines were a constant hazard during the war and one was observed by the coastguard on duty at Llanddwyn at 10.00am on 17 October 1941. The mine was driven on to nearby rocks close to the lighthouse and the resulting explosion at 4.30pm damaged the door and roof of the lighthouse and smashed four windows. Several more drifting mines were observed on 6 January 1942, some driven ashore at Llanddwyn and Abermenai beach and one drifting into the Strait but they were all rendered ineffective by the mine disposal officer of the Admiralty.

On 4 May 1943 the Harbour Trust took delivery of a light fire-fighting trailer pump for use within the port area, and further precautions had to be taken such as the camouflage of the oil tanks adjoining the Victoria Dock, so as to be 'invisible' from the air. With the possibility of oil supplies being disrupted by enemy action additional tanks were installed underground at the old brickworks at *Parkia*, Griffiths Crossing and on 5 August 1941 petrol started to be pumped from Caernarvon, through a 4" pipe laid by the War Department, to the new Shell depot where a petrol can filling facility had been installed. Thereafter, whenever a delivery of petrol was made to Caernarvon by ship, it was immediately pumped through to Griffiths Crossing. These new oil installations enabled high octane petrol, suitable for planes, to be stored prior to distribution to nearby airfields. A periodic inspection of the sea outlets took place at Griffiths Crossing by the Harbour Trust and the Fisheries Patrol Officer for signs of oil pollution into the Strait.

The facilities provided at Port Dinorwic dry-dock together with the workforce expertise were used extensively during the war with many vessels, especially those damaged by enemy action, being repaired.

At nearby Dinas, Port Dinorwic, the Dowsett Engineering Construction Co. Ltd. (or Dow-Mac as it was generally known) had taken over the old shipbuilding yard and erected a large shed over it. There they assembled steel sections to form 40 foot, flat-bottomed tugs powered by a twin screw petrol engine and a small open wheelhouse aft for towing barges of similar size for use as supply boats in the Persian Gulf waterways. When completed, sea trials were held against a measured mile between Rowen Bay, Felinheli and Llanfairisgaer along the Menai Strait. The barges were then stacked along the foreshore at Felinheli (Port Dinorwic) prior to being transported by low-loader to Liverpool for onward shipment. Steel sections for the barges were stored at Ala Las, and St Helens Road, Caernarvon.

Red Cross Parcels Group at the Caernarfon Drill Hall.
[Mrs Doris Rogers]

CHAPTER 12: Voluntary Work and Entertainment

Comforts for the Troops

Comforts committees formed in most towns and villages were able to organise the distribution of wool to those who had both the time and the expertise to knit woollen garments for the troops. These garments were produced for members of the forces stationed in the locality or specifically for individuals serving in other places. They were always welcomed by members of the forces especially when tours of duty were conducted during the winter months. Letters of thanks were received by the Anglesey Comforts Committee on 19 May 1943 from 'C' Battery 130 Royal Artillery, Llanfwrog thanking them for woollen comforts and similarly from 4th Heavy Anti-Aircraft Training Camp at Ty Croes. [PNP 481]

The *War Knitting and Wool Book* describes the items knitted as mittens, socks, helmets or cap comforter and scarves. They were made from sombre grey, navy or khaki coloured wool mostly contributed by the knitters themselves or purchased from funds raised for the purpose. Staff and pupils of the County School at Caernarvon contributed towards the knitting and supply of comforts on a regular basis. [GAS - X/DI 736] A newspaper report stated that by the end of the war the Port Dinorwic Knitting Class had supplied 3,146 garments in 151 parcels for the forces. [C&DH 12.10.45]

To help relieve the boredom of military life, arrangements were made between the Army Bureau of Current Affairs (ABCA), being part of the Army Education Project, who were responsible for twenty-three areas in the United Kingdom, and the University College of North Wales to provide about one hundred lecturers, who were paid £1.1/- per lecture, willing to travel and give talks to members of the armed forces wherever they were stationed. One of the lecturers was G P Wells the son of H G Wells. When lecturers travelled in their own cars they were provided with extra petrol coupons; at other times they were taken to their destination by WVS drivers. Since it was possible to have as many as forty-three lectures in any evening in an area extending from Harlech to Denbigh including the island of Anglesey, it entailed a great deal of planning for the Education Officer. It was necessary therefore for each unit to be supplied with a list of possible subjects and, whenever possible, a programme of lectures would be planned for about 8 to 9 weeks ahead. Similar talks were also given by women who would talk to WAAFs, ATS and WRENs about dress materials etc.

The various airfields, Anti-Aircraft Gun sites, Searchlight Units, Naval Stations, Maintenance Units etc. put requests for talks about a variety of subjects. Not all members of the forces would welcome the lectures; many of those on airfields and other garrisons often had alternative forms of entertainment. Possibly the men who appreciated the talks most of all were small units of six to eight who manned the Anti-Aircraft ('Ack Ack') Gun sites.

National Savings Committees

The public were given every encouragement to save and a band of dedicated collectors would go from house to house each week selling savings stamps which, when sufficient had been collected, could be exchanged for a National Savings Certificate. Although the rate of interest at that time was very low the savers felt that the contributions were towards a good cause.

As a further incentive towards saving, support would be given by a town or county towards a nationally declared project such as *Wings for Victory* or *Warships* week and duly acknowledged with the appropriate name being applied to the aeroplane or vessel being

'purchased'.[GAS WM/316/9] When the county of Caernarvon raised the necessary funds a Mk IIb Spitfire (P8690) was named *Caernarvonshire* and allocated to 12 MU on 25 May 1941 before being taken over by 610 Squadron 3 June 1941 and 616 Squadron on 19 July 1941. Sadly, it failed to return from operations on 21 July 1941. Merioneth was equally successful in raising funds for a Mk I Spitfire (R7136) and similarly named. It was flown by test pilot George Pickering on 18 February 1941 before being transferred to 12 MU on 5 March 1941, followed by 124 Squadron on 7 May 1941, 340 Squadron 20 October 1941 and 52 OTU, 9 December 1941. It was involved in a Category B flying accident on 15 April 1942, transferred to AST (Hamble), 7 November 1942 and 'struck off charge' on 23 November 1942.

British Red Cross Society

In addition to its traditional role as nursing staff, the British Red Cross Society also arranged and administered the packing of food parcels containing standard items such as tea, sugar, cigarettes, tinned fruit, corned beef, and which were distributed to British POWs held on the Continent. By 1944 the weekly output of parcels from the UK had reached 102,000. [PNP219]

Women's Voluntary Service

With war looming on the horizon the Dowager Marchioness of Reading was asked by the Home Secretary, Sir Samuel Hoare, on 16 May 1938 to form an organisation to assist local authorities with the recruitment of women for the Women's Voluntary Service (later to become the Women's Royal Voluntary Service) for Air Raid Precautions. By September 1939, when the title was changed to 'Women's Voluntary Service for Civil Defence', the WVS, as it was generally known, had in excess of 300,000 volunteers but, within a few months this had increased to 1,000,000.

Amongst the many functions carried out by the WVS was that of organising the welfare of evacuees, clothing exchanges and distribution of gift clothing from America. Rather than discard clothing, especially of growing children, it was not unusual for families to exchange articles that would fit another generation so that none went to waste during times of austerity and utility. The WVS also ran mobile canteens for emergency feeding, manned enquiry points, worked in rest centres and organised volunteer car pools. Its well-stocked mobile library and canteen often brought a little cheer to British soldiers stuck on a remote and lonely gun-site so relieving what was often a tedious vigil.

The salvage scheme produced a mass of saucepans, kettles and jelly moulds for the essential aluminium desperately needed in the manufacture of fighter aircraft. Indeed, the WVS was so well organised that they were quite capable of arranging the collection of any article or material specified by the Government as being in short supply. They were also given the task by the Ministry of Works and Planning of visiting some 2,000 farms and derelict sites over a matter of weeks looking for scrap iron.

Peace may have brought about a cessation of hostilities, but the suffering which the people had stoically endured did not end as dramatically as the war had with the bombing of Japan. The plight of the families who had lost their homes and possessions and having to cope with the on-going rationing and shortage of coal, added to the misery of very cold winters. Electricity cuts did nothing to ease the plight of the sick, old and infirm left shivering at home with blankets and rugs and the mediocre light from a candle. To ease the problem, the WVS organised the Household Gifts scheme whereby people who had not been affected by the bombs were asked to donate

'War Weapons Week' Parade, Caernarfon. Members of the
Womens Army Corps march past the War Memorial in
Castle Square, followed by a contingent from the
British Red Cross.
[Gwynedd Archives Service]

A detachment from the United States Army march through Castle
Square, Caernarfon on a 'Salute the Soldier' Parade.
Note the old Herald Offices in the background.
[Mr Stuart Whiskin]

A detachment of Army Cadets march through Castle Square,
Caernarfon during a 'War Bonds' Parade, 1944.
[Mr R T Jones]

The Wrens, followed by a detachment of Royal Naval officers,
march through Castle Square, Caernarfon during the
'Salute the Soldier' Parade.
[Mr Stuart Whiskin]

kitchen utensils and furniture. Not only did the people of this country respond but gifts also came from Canada, USA, Australia, New Zealand, Ecuador, Argentine and Chile providing blankets, Switzerland with furniture, Nigeria with cotton cloth and India supplying linen and floor rugs. It took eighteen months to distribute the gifts to 111,075 families.

With the rebuilding of houses at the end of the war and in particular with the erecting of prefabricated bungalows, the WVS organised the Garden Gift Scheme in 1946 whereby people with well established gardens contributed plants and seeds for use in the barren ground around these new houses and on bombed sites. Seeds, both of flowers and vegetables, were also sent by horticultural societies from the USA.

Throughout the UK, two hundred and forty-one members of the WVS were killed during the war.

Entertainment

Fearing immediate air-raids when war was declared, the Government ordered the closure of all places of public entertainment and sports stadia on 4 September 1939 as it was thought that many casualties would be caused if bombs dropped on such places where large numbers of people might be concentrated. However, they did not remain shut for long as the Government realised that entertainment was an excellent morale booster during wartime. Such was the popularity of the cinema that people queued stoically in the dark whatever the weather, waiting patiently for a vacant seat. A great many adults saw at least one film a week, sometimes more, during the war. Most war-time films had an element of morale boosting running through them and some propaganda thrown in for good measure. Whenever possible, people still took a seaside holiday even though access to the sea was precluded because of anti-invasion measures as was the case at Dinas Dinlle near Caernarvon.

CHAPTER 13: 'Mulberry Harbour'

The Prime Minister, Mr (later Sir) Winston Churchill, was noted for his memoranda and one in particular set out his requirements for the intended invasion of Europe.

"Piers for use on Beaches – They must float up and down with the tide. The anchor problem must be mastered. Let me have the best solution worked out. Don't argue the matter. The difficulties will argue for themselves. 30.5.1942".

It was agreed by the Combined Chiefs of Staff in May 1943 that a full-scale attack had to be undertaken across the Channel within twelve months. Undoubtedly Churchill had envisaged many of the problems that could be encountered not least of all the supply of ammunition, petrol and food and the means of transport from the beaches. On the assumption that it would be unlikely that the Germans would leave ports in Brittany and Normandy intact for the benefit of invading troops, a way had to be found to ensure that supplies would flow across the Channel and into France unimpeded.

Even when it was eventually decided that supplies would be delivered on to open beaches, the possibility of adverse weather, even in the summer-time, curtailing or even preventing deliveries, had to be borne in mind (as it happened, an unseasonable storm did indeed occur). For this reason, the decision was made to provide an artificial harbour.

Following on the instruction issued by the Prime Minister, Lord

Mountbatten asked British engineers for plans of a suitable artificial harbour bearing in mind the shallow sand sea-bed, such as is common on the Normandy coast, and the fact that the piers were to be designed to carry the heaviest tanks and artillery. Of three schemes submitted, one was by Mr H Iorys Hughes, a professional consulting engineer, and he was instructed by Headquarters Combined Operations to design and proceed with the construction of prototypes in June 1942.

The first intimation that the town of Conwy would be involved in the construction of what were to be known as 'Mulberry Harbours' came on 28 October 1942 when Mr H E West, a representative of Messrs Holloway Bros. (London) Ltd., Builders and Contractors, called to see the Town Clerk. West brought with him a letter from Iorys Hughes by way of introduction and indicating that he intended to make use of a piece of land on the Morfa for constructional purposes. Hughes asked permission for West to make trial borings so as to examine the subsoil. The letter also referred to '... the derelict house known as 'The Beacons'...' and that '... it would be of great use in the proposed works...'

The work to be carried out on the Morfa was described as being a "vital secret and of Prime Minister priority". It required a frontage on to the foreshore of 1,150 feet in front of the Beacons (but to keep the compensation to a figure of £6 per annum, the land was described as 'very sandy and of little agricultural value'). It was anticipated that the first group of men would start work within a fortnight and some 200 workmen would be on site within three weeks and that eventually 1,000 would be employed. It was also suggested that Bryn Corach, Beechwood Court, Conwy be taken over initially for accommodation and two rooms would be requisitioned in 'South Beacons' for the storage of implements. The resident engineer was Mr E W Etcheles. [GAS XB2/454]

Iorys Hughes arrived on the 30 October 1942 together with Captain Coulson of the War Department and together they produced a plan showing the land required on the Morfa fronting Deganwy together with part of the land leased to Caernarvonshire Golf Club. Work was to start on the site on 2 November 1942 with the building of a new road by Conwy Borough Council on behalf of Holloway Bros. At the same time, discussion took place as to the cost to Holloway Bros. of their vehicles crossing the suspension bridge at Conwy (contract 294/27/R421).

In his letter of the 10 April 1943 the Minister of War Transport writing from the Empire Hotel, Blackpool, to the Town Clerk, Conwy, referred to the construction by the War Department of fourteen launching ways on the foreshore and river bed adjacent to 'The Beacons'. A telephone message was received stating that the "... first concrete barge was to be launched Tuesday 4 May 1943 at 12.10 and it will be necessary for the harbour to be closed to all navigation on that date..."

There is a record of a message being received on 18 June 1943 from Mr West of Holloway Bros. stating "... that he expected to complete the work on the land adjoining the Beacons and to clear all materials away next week..." (a letter received on 13 September 1943 referred to a new contract on the Morfa – from 'Sam Parry's Bridge across the Golf Links to the Beacons'). On 8 March 1944 a message was received by the Town Clerk from Mr West stating that "... they would be launching one of their boats built by Joseph Parkes Ltd. tomorrow (Thursday) between 11 and 12 o'clock..." (no name was ever given to the components under construction until the 'Whale Project' was mentioned in a letter to the Borough Council on 21 December 1943. Reference to the 'Mulberry Harbour' was not made until the 20 September 1945 when the removal of the concrete anchor points, cables and chains, installed by Holloway Bros. in the River Conwy, was under discussion by the Council after complaints had been received from yachtsmen).

In August 1943 a mission left the UK for the Quebec Conference to assist in planning the final 'Mulberry Harbours' and on 27 August 1943 the War Office was instructed to start urgent plans into the possibility of constructing caissons and, accordingly asked Mr Iorys Hughes to commence investigations. When the final decision was taken to use the War Office design rather than his own, he was asked whether he was prepared to continue advising on the whole scheme. His reaction was:

"Being more skilled and experienced than anyone I knew of, and it being a war effort, I agreed and entered into things wholeheartedly..."

In a letter sent by Iorys Hughes from his offices at 66 Victoria Street, Westminster, SW1 dated 28.9.43 and marked 'Most Secret' he stated:

"The instructions received are that it is proposed to construct monoliths at points to be selected on the south coast and to float them by launching. The proportions of the monoliths would be up to 5,000 tons displacement, draught from 8 to 18 feet, and some 180 to 200 feet in length ... (and) to side-launch (rather than end-launch)..."

The steel plates, which were used for the pier-heads, were pre-assembled by riveting or welding sections at the Joseph Parkes & Son works at Northwich and transported on articulated lorries to the Morfa. At the berths, the steelwork was placed in position by large cranes and welded together. Other construction firms involved included Holloway Bros., Waring & Co. and Ace Welders Ltd., all from London.

At its busiest, 900 men and women, worked 24 hours a day in twelve hour shifts, on the Mulberry project at Conwy and such was the pressure for the work to be completed that blackout regulations were ignored. This army of workers transformed a quiet and secluded corner of the Morfa covering about ten acres, including part of the golf course, into a hive of activity whilst the administrative staff were housed in the nearby property known as *The Beacons*.

To counter the effect of adverse weather on the workers, protective clothing was supplied and the canteens were kept busy providing hot drinks. The men, working seven days a week with no mention of days off or holiday, were housed at hostels, holiday homes and boarding houses, indeed anywhere where there was a bed to spare. Even convalescent homes were pressed into service when accommodation was required. Buses would tour the various lodging houses to collect the men for work and return them at the end of the shift.

The Mulberry harbour design called for a number of floating pier-

A 'Mulberry Harbour' pierhead after launching at Morfa Conwy.
[North Wales Chronicle]

A 'Mulberry Harbour' off the coast of Normandy, during the summer of 1944.
[Mr Malcolm H D McAlpine]

heads to be moored off the beach and connected to it by means of floating bridges with a line of breakwater giving protection from the sea. Such a breakwater would reduce the waves and allow small launches and amphibious vehicles to operate inside the harbour and ships and LSTs to discharge their cargo.

There have been attempts at attributing the design of the Mulberry Harbour to various individuals but the answer given to a question in the House of Commons 8 November 1944 made the situation no clearer:

"In a work of such magnitude, many persons were naturally engaged ... (including) Civil Engineers and consultants, notably Messrs. Gwyther, Iorys Hughes, Lobnitz and Kent, contributed to the design..."

Although Iorys Hughes had been asked to accept a temporary senior rank in the Royal Engineers, he made the following observation:

"I [Iorys Hughes] would be more useful and my word would carry more weight if I remained a civilian ... I was paid for my services a very reduced professional fee, which scarcely covered the cost of my staff and overheads. I finished the war worse off financially and three stones lighter!. When the War Office asked whether I was prepared to accept a reduced fee I accepted the reduction due to my wish not to be thought a 'war profiteer'..."

Hugh Iorys Hughes, described as a man of action, was born in Bangor, North Wales in 1902 into a family which had been connected with shipping for several generations. He was educated at Friars School, Bangor and at Sheffield University where he obtained a First Class Honours Degree in Civil Engineering. Although only a few miles from his home, the work carried out at Conwy was done in the utmost secrecy, and even those closest to him and working with him had no idea of the purpose of his construction. For those who were directly involved with the Mulberry Harbour, it was felt that he had not been given sufficient credit for his contribution to his involvement with the floating pier-heads and the towing design for the units.

Some 45,000 men were to be involved throughout the UK in the construction of the various components of the Mulberry harbour, responsible for landing 40% of equipment and personnel on the beachhead in Normandy, and the enormity of the operation can best be judged by looking at the cost involved. If the same operation had to be mounted today, Franklin & Andrews, the quantity surveyors which costed the Mulberry project, estimate that at today's prices, the project would cost £1,000 million.

Chapter 14: Conclusions

With the cessation of hostilities came celebrations which took on many forms. Bonfires, carefully built in eager anticipation, were lit and could be seen on the top of many hills. The Victory Parades, concerts and street parties for the children that followed were enjoyed by those who participated but, to others, the events merely emphasised a void within a family for, sadly, many of those who had departed to serve their country were not to return.

Those who had served in the forces impatiently waited for their demobilisation, which entailed being given a free civilian utility suit in a limited choice of colour and style, in order that they could return home and resume some sort of normality.

It would take many more months before rationing was discontinued and the empty shop shelves began to be filled. The

importation of food and war materials was governed by the number of ships available and home production controlled by availability of manpower and conversion from war to peace production. Advice on cooking continued to be given by the Ministry of Food and it extolled the virtues of certain foods, especially potatoes which were readily available.

Mr (later Lord) Goronwy Roberts MP addressing the Port Dinorwic (Clwb y Fenai) youth club in September 1945 stated that the Government had the task of turning the war industry into peace production, reviving the economy and creating full employment. He prophesied that in a few years "...there was more work available than workmen...".

Even when employment was available at the end of the war, there was a tendency to pick and choose. Farmers attending the Hiring Fair at Pwllheli in May 1945 found that unemployed skilled farm workers were reluctant to return to their pre-war employment even at a wage of £3.10s per week.

The Snowdon Mountain Railway restarted operations on 7 May 1945 and charabanc trips, which had been popular before the war, restarted as buses and staff became available. The Caernarvon Football Club was reformed in October 1945 and, a couple of months later, after six years of inactivity, the Caernarvon Mixed Choir celebrated their first concert under their conductor Miss Dilys Wynne Williams. The Crosville Male Voice choir, which had performed regularly during the war, under the baton of Mr Richard Jones, joined other artistes in a concert at the *Majestic Cinema*, Caernarvon September 1945 to celebrate the end of the war. In the same month the senior pupils of Caernarvon Grammar School gave a performance of Oscar Wilde's *The Importance of Being Earnest* directed by Mrs Nancy Bingley and Mr S A Claridge. The London, Midland & Scottish (LMS) Railway restarted dining car rolling stock on to the North Wales line "with cutlery replated" on 1 October 1945. The North Wales Agricultural Show, suspended since 1938, restarted at the Oval in Caernarvon on 8 November 1945 and "... attracted a bumper gate...".

The naval camp, HMS *Glendower*, was under discussion by members of the County Council as a possible venue for an educational establishment in preference to a holiday camp. But it would appear that the eventual holiday camp was a foregone conclusion irrespective of the fact that many representations were made to the Government. [GAS XM/6615/94] [*C&DH* 9.11.45]

In September 1945, 300 uniformed members of the Land Army marched past the Lord Lieutenant of Caernarvonshire, Brigadier W H Wynne Finch who took the salute at the University College of North Wales, Bangor. Later at the Powis Hall, Hugh Owen, chairman of the Caernarvonshire War Executive Committee, thanked the girls "... for a difficult job well done...". The following month the 6th Bn Royal Welch Fusiliers were honoured with the Freedom of the Borough of Caernarvon.

Drifting mines, sometimes dislodged by gales, were always a menace along the coast and one such object which drifted on to Llanfairfechan beach on 4 January 1943 was made harmless by the army. [GAS XJ 2366] Another caused the residents of Rhosneigr to be evacuated in September 1945 when it drifted on to nearby rocks. Mines, unexploded bombs and other war-time debris were to be a hazard for many years after the war.

Inevitably, after fifty years, the memory of the war years begins to fade but, for those who spent the greater part of their time working long hours in factories, very few, if any, grumbled about the hard work. Invariably they recall the camaraderie that existed making it "the best years of our lives".

Appendix I: Aerial Attacks

Two parachute mines were dropped on the Maesgeirchen housing estate outside Bangor at 8.44pm on 24 October 1941 – one at the top of Penrhyn Avenue which formed a large crater in the road measuring 26 feet diameter by 10 feet deep, and the other near the 15th tee of Bangor Golf Club. Two houses were demolished and one man and one woman killed, with 14 injured. Twenty nine houses were damaged to such an extent that they could not be occupied and a further 170 damaged to a lesser extent. The furniture from these houses were stored in the old Woolworth's building and various chapel vestries in town until such time as they had been repaired. The homeless were found temporary accommodation and food was provided at *Robert Roberts Café* and by the WVS at the 'Rest Centre'. [GAS XM/797/4]

The raider that came over Conwy on 13 March 1941, dropped bombs causing "… slight damage to 28 houses (costing £15 to repair) and injuring three persons who were taken to hospital". [GAS XB2/79]

German aircraft dropped a stick of nine bombs on the mountain between Llanfairfechan and Aber on 8 September 1940 which resulted in no more than a series of craters. A further visit was made by enemy aircraft to the Llanfairfechan district on 19 October 1940, and sixty-five incendiary bombs were dropped in a twenty minute raid but no damage was caused. In an another incident shortly afterwards a member of the public reported to the police that a parachute had been discovered on the Llanfairfechan beach. When examined it was found to be of German origin and with a number of ropes attached. It was deduced that if a bomb or land mine had been attached then it had buried itself in the sand! [GAS XJ2363]

On Tuesday 24 September 1940 as the result of bombs being dropped in a raid on Llanllechid near Bethesda, the bakery in the High Street was damaged and the property Llwyn Derw in Water Street was demolished. There were four occupants in Llwyn Derw at the time; one woman was killed and three persons were admitted to the Caernarvon & Anglesey Infirmary at Bangor at 10.30pm: Mrs Mary Davies (age 35) and Dilys Davies (age 12) both suffered scalp wounds & Ronald Davies (age 11) had abrasions (one of the children subsequently died). On the same evening, incendiary bombs were dropped in the garden of 69 Carneddi Road, Bethesda but little damage was done. Of the six flares dropped on Llanberis, one landed on the Snowdon Mountain Railway platform and the others on the mountain-side. There were also reports of bombs being dropped between Nantlle and Drws-y-Coed. [GAS XC12/1/6 & XC12/1/168]

A parachute mine was dropped at Efa Lwyd Fawr on the outskirts of Penygroes 20 December 1940 but the force of the resulting explosion was nullified to a certain extent because the soft ground and nearby hill absorbed most of the energy. However, it still left sufficient force to destroy a number of windows in the area including that of Calfaria Chapel.

Possibly, because of its closeness to Penrhos airfield, a number of bombs were dropped on the outskirts of Pwllheli and the town also suffered an aerial machine gun attack on the town square when some shops were damaged. A Heinkel 111 was shot down near the Pwllheli golf links 30 July 1942 and two of its crew were rescued from the sea. A further two members of the crew who were drowned, were buried in Pwllheli cemetary. [GAS XC12/1/103]

Between 9 July 1940 and 24 July 1941, 131 High Explosive bombs were dropped in Caernarvonshire and of these 24 failed to explode. In the same period one parachute mine was dropped and approximately 271 Incendiary Bombs.

Holyhead was subjected to a number of bombing attacks including one when there was a Canadian ammunition ship at Salt Island unloading on to a train which was standing in the station. Had either the ship or the train been hit, the resulting explosion would have been catastrophic.

Other recorded incidents on Anglesey were (courtesy of G W Brown):

Date	Location	Nature of Explosives
12.7.40	Holyhead	2 Parachute mines. Ship sunk. 11 dead, 3 seriously hurt.
4.9.40	Llanfachraeth	Incendiary Bombs
5.9.40	Llandegfan	Incendiary Bombs
5.10.40	Holyhead	6 High Explosives, 20 Incendiary Bombs. 3 Seriously and 3 slightly hurt Church House demolished 90 houses slightly damaged.
10.10.40	Llangadwaldr	Incendiary Bombs
6.11.40	Llanfachraeth	Incendiary Bombs
8.11.40	Holyhead	4 High Explosive (3 in harbour) 1 unexploded 1100lb bomb dug up.
11.11.40	Penmon Quarry	3 High Explosives
2.1.41	Holland Arms	2 Parachute Mines, 1 Unexploded Parachute Mine. 3 slight casualties. 10 houses badly damaged.
12.1.41	Amlwch	Machine Gun Bullets.
13.1.41	Holyhead	Machine Gunned
25.2.41	Holyhead	2 Parachute Mines Salt Island 11 slight casualties 17 houses badly damaged 250 houses slightly damaged.
11.3.41	Mynydd Bodafon Llanfihangel	1 High Explosive Bomb 1 High Explosive Bomb
12.3.41	Llanfair PG	6 High Explosive Bombs 2 light casualties 1 house demolished and 1 badly damaged
12.3.41	Holyhead	2 Parachute Mines outside harbour.
14.3.41	Plas Newydd Llanfair PG	2 High Explosive Bombs.
6.4.41	Holyhead	2 Parachute Mines out harbour
7.4.41	Dalar Cross Roads	Incendiary Bombs
9.4.41	Holyhead	8 High Explosive and Incendiary Bombs 2 in harbour, 1 unexploded bomb Wesleyan Chapel damaged 11 houses badly damaged 144 houses slightly damaged
6.5.41	Holyhead	3 High Explosive - outer harbour.
7.5.41	Holyhead	4 Parachute Mines - harbour closed
9.5.41	Holyhead	Machine gun Bullets.

Bomb damage opposite the railway station, Land's End, Holyhead, 9 April 1941.
[Mr G W Brown]

Bomb crater at Newry, Holyhead, 1941.
[Mr G W Brown]

		Bomber brought down in sea beyond Porthdafarch, Holyhead.
10.5.41	Holyhead	3 High Explosive bombs. 2 slight casualties F.A. Post (Sailors Home) 25 houses damaged, 50 slightly damaged
31.5.41	Llandegfan	1 High Explosive - shore of Menai Strait.
24.7.41	Aberffraw	2 High Explosive bombs 4 sheep killed
	Bodedern	1 High Explosive Bomb
	Llanfaethlu	1 High Explosive Bomb
24.10.41	Pen-yr-Argae	2 Parachute Mines
	Llanfachraeth	4 houses slightly damaged.
1.11.41	Heneglwys	1 High Explosive Bomb. 2 unexploded High Explosive Bombs
		Enemy bomber shot down.

APPENDIX II: Bomb Clearance

Llanberis

From the outbreak of war, the roads above Llanberis and in the vicinity of storage areas, had been controlled by the RAF and the only members of the public who were allowed to use them were those whose property could only be accessed from such roads, and they were granted special passes. When it was decided that roads along the mountain-side and skirting the storage area, would be reopened by the Air Ministry to the public, suitable fences were erected in an attempt at preventing anyone from entering the potentially dangerous quarries or pits which had been used in the disposal of the bombs. In practice however, those of a more determined character found such precautions a mere hindrance and, in the succeeding years, the fence was breached on several occasions.

Discussions took place periodically as to the security of the area and the possibility of clearing the pits of remaining explosives but, this was dismissed as being 'hazardous and uneconomical'. Owing to the presence of explosives and the constant source of anxiety to those responsible for the area, HQ Maintenance Command was given the task of conducting a reconnaissance of the pits area in 1969. No. 71 MU Bomb Disposal Flight, later renamed No 2 Explosives Ordnance Depot Unit, found evidence of excavation and removal of explosives from Pit Area No 4. This discovery and the forthcoming investiture of the Prince of Wales prompted the Ministry of Defence to take action.

By May 1970 Pit No. 1, had been given clearance from all dangerous devices and, within two years a similar clearance was given to Pit No. 4. Similar work continued on Pit No. 3 and interconnecting tunnels. As the result of a survey carried out by naval frogmen, a large quantity of derelict explosives had been found in the lake in Pit 2C. With the assistance of No. 38 Engineering Regiment RE who were responsible for civil engineering support, including building roads to various pits, 20 million gallons of water had to be pumped out of the lake before work on the removal of the explosives could begin. With the removal of the water, it became apparent that it would take at least two years to dispose of all that had been revealed.

Whilst the quarries were being cleared, a radio link was maintained between Llanberis and RAF Valley where a Casevac helicopter and medical personnel could be summoned if an accident occurred.

Although many hazards and difficulties were encountered, the final clearance and handing over of the site to the Property Services Agency was achieved on 31 October 1975 for eventual disposal (PRO - 31MU Llanberis 29/994).

Llandwrog

When the Allied forces occupied Germany in 1945 and discovered a large dump of nerve gas bombs, the decision was taken for part of the consignment to be taken to the United States of America and the remainder to the United Kingdom. At that time the war in the Far East was still continuing and there was the possibility that these bombs could be used against Japan. Initially, the UK share of 71,000 GA bombs (each of 330lbs and containing 190lbs of the nerve gas Tabun) was brought to the port of Hamburg to be loaded from the dockside on to vessels, such as the *Empire Condor*, to be shipped to Newport, South Wales.

On arrival in Newport the ship was isolated from all other vessels and, apart from the civilian crane operator, only RAF personnel of 6 Explosives Unit were permitted to be in the vicinity whilst the bombs were being transferred from ship to railway wagons. Even customs officials were not allowed to be involved. The train, made up of some twenty-four wagons with a similar number of bombs in each wagon, took three days to travel to Llanberis because it was restricted to travelling at night when there were fewer other trains about. During daylight hours, whilst the train was in railway sidings away from any built-up area and guarded by RAF personnel, a fresh train crew would take over for the next stage of the journey. It took approximately nine months for all the bombs to be transferred in this manner.

On arrival at Llanberis the bombs were transferred on to Dodge or Scammel lorries and a convoy of eight to ten of these vehicles, driven by civilians dressed in anti-gas clothing, travelled three or four times a day to Llandwrog accompanied by a decontamination unit lorry, fire tender and RAF motor cyclists as escort. When all the wagons had been emptied and the bombs transferred to the airfield, the RAF personnel returned to Newport by passenger train in time to bring the next consignment to Llanberis.

Until 1945, Llandwrog airfield had been the scene of much air activity but its reversion to a peacetime role at the end of the war was delayed when it was taken over by 277 MU, part of the Bicester based 42 Group, responsible for the storing of the bombs on the airfield. These, contained in their original boxes of about 6 feet long by 2 feet square with German identification marks, were stacked on the runways, four high and guarded as a Class A security area by RAF personnel with guard dogs. [Disposal of German Chemical Warfare Stocks COS (45) 400 (0) and PRO WO193/712]

The Arrival and Departure register of the Caernarvon Harbour Trust (the body responsible for all maritime movement in the Menai Strait) gives some indication of the activity involved with the airfield and its extended military use. In the latter part of 1946 and the beginning of 1947 there are references to various craft delivering cargoes described as steel hangars for RAF Llandwrog. [GAS XD15/8/8a]

A further entry recorded by the Trust on 7 January 1947 stated:

"...two cargoes consisting of airodrome (sic) Hangars for the RAF station at Llandwrog. I am informed that several more of these hangars will be imported in the near future. Some trouble was experienced in getting efficient labour to discharge these vessels but this has now been overcome and quite a good gang of men were engaged on the last ship and can be secured for other ships in the future..."

A rather indistinct photograph showing the gas bombs stored at RAF Llandwrog c1946.
[Caernarvon & Denbigh Herald]

Loading gas bombs on to LCTs near Belan Fort, Caernarfon, c1954.
[Caernarvon & Denbigh Herald]

Loading gas bombs on to LCTs near Belan Fort, Caernarfon, c1954.
[Caernarvon & Denbigh Herald]

These continuing operations and movement of military vessels taking place along the Menai Strait in the years following on the Second World War, were not all recorded at the Harbour office but noted in the minute book of the Trust merely as 'confidential matters'.

By 1951, twenty-four Belman hangars had been erected on the runways with twenty-three of them used to house the bombs previously stacked on the runway and one for servicing and checking for leakages. During the time when they were in storage each case was opened to check the condition of the bomb and ensure that no leakage was occurring. Gas masks and suitable outer clothing were worn during the checking operation and the latter discarded as soon as it was taken off, whether leakages were found or not.

The few that were found to be leaking were dealt with by a team of six civilians. The defective items were placed on planks above a pit four feet square and twelve feet deep, into which caustic soda was poured from barrels until three quarters filled. A civilian armourer would unscrew a plug from the leaking bomb allowing the contents to be poured into the pit where it would be neutralised by the soda.

Working in protective clothing during such operations, made the men perspire profusely and so a shift would be restricted to two hours in the morning and a similar length in the afternoon. At the end of the two hour stage they attended the decontamination centre where they went through a shower to remove any possible contamination from the bomb on their outer clothing. After undressing, every piece of clothing was burnt; it was never used a second time. Following on a further shower they had an opportunity of relaxing before the next shift.

Each member of the squad handling the bombs was examined by a local doctor and given blood tests every six weeks to ensure that there had been no contamination from the gas. If any was detected it would entail coming off the job for six weeks by which time the effect of the gas would have worn off. For this type of work they received three shillings a day (15p) danger money. Lectures were given periodically to emphasise the care required in handling the bombs and the possible danger from the gas contained inside.

The ending of the Second World War brought the problem of disposing of large quantities of munitions, both explosive and chemical. As far as the gas bombs stored at Llandwrog were concerned, various ways of disposal were considered, but in the end it was concluded that deep sea burial would be the most satisfactory from the point of view of cost, time and safety. The site chosen was about 250 miles west of Colonsay in the Outer Hebrides and the undertaking was given the name 'Operation Sandcastle'.

The first task was to reduce the length of the bombs from approximately six feet to four feet by removing the fins with the aid of a guillotine and, correspondingly, the wooden containers. They were taken on small flat-topped Bantam lorries along a specially built road to a concrete landing strip near Belan Fort. There they were unloaded with the aid of gravity-fed rollers on to Royal Navy Auxiliary Fleet, Landing Craft Transport (LCT) twin-screw vessels of about 180 feet long. [GAS XD15/39/131]

The empty craft, with its crew of eight and two airmen personnel, was guided by a pilot through the Strait, but when loaded with the bombs its voyage to Cairnryan near Stranraer was always undertaken around Anglesey.

On arrival at Belan Fort, the LCT, under the directions of beachmasters (who were usually retired naval men) would drop a ramp on to a purpose built concrete apron enabling fork lift vehicles to load each vessel with approximately 480 bombs. Up to five of these vessels were used on the run between Belan Fort and Cairnryan and loading was undertaken immediately after arrival of an LCT irrespective of the time of day or night. In the latter case, arc lights were used with small portable electric generators supplying the power.

Although there were times when the beachmaster would decide against the voyage to Cairnryan because of adverse weather, when conditions and tides were favourable, it was feasible to dispatch two loaded vessels in a day. Stern anchors were used on occasions to assist in getting off the beach but the power of the engines was usually sufficient. However, as an additional precaution, an auxiliary naval tug with civilian crew was usually ready to assist whenever a craft was expected or departing.

The LCT with a speed of eight to nine knots, took sixteen to eighteen hours to cover the journey from Fort Belan to Cairnryan. If the conditions were favourable, it usually took about three days for the loaded craft to travel to Cairnryan, unload and return. Most of the voyages took place in the summer months between May and September because the flat-bottomed vessel had difficulty in coping with rough seas. On arrival at Cairnryan, the bombs were unloaded on to one side of a military jetty and reloaded on the other side on to an old cargo steamship. The operation to clear the bombs from Llandwrog took approximately eighteen months and was completed by 1955.

Although there must have been a virtual continual movement through the Strait for about 18 months of War Transport vessels, few entries appear in the Arrival and Departure register. Even when an entry is made as with the arrival of Motor Vessel (MV) ADC 442 on 8 January 1955 under Captain Ross and departing shortly after for Cairnryan, the cargo being carried merely refers to 'Company RASC' [GAS – XD15/6/9]. The question of a charge to be levied against Royal Army Service Corps (War Transport) (RASC W/T) vessels using berthing facilities in the (Victoria) dock was under discussion by the Trust on 5 July 1955 and it was decided that it would be £1 per vessel per berth. [GAS D/15/2/4]

BIBLIOGRAPHY

Beauman, Katherine Bentley, *Greensleeves - WVS/WRVS* (Seeley Service & Co.) 1977

Beddoe, Deidre & Leigh Verrill-Rhys, *Parachutes and Petticoats* (Honno Autobiography) 1992

Bridges, Frank, *Saunders Roe Ltd.*1948

Brown, Winifred, *No Distress Signals* (Peter Davies Ltd.) 1952

Doylerush, Edward, *Fallen Eagles* (Midland Counties Publications) 1990

Doylerush, Edward, *No Landing Place* (Midland Counties Publications) 1985

Fay, Leonard G., *Sea Breezes* magazine 'Career of the Conway'

Freeman, Roger A., *Britain at War* (Arms and Armour Press) 1990

Geary, W., *Notes on Farming* 1949

Graham, Virginia, *The Story of the WVS* (HMSO) 1959

Harrison, Michael, *Mulberry – the Return in Triumph* (W H Allen) 1965

Hartcup, Guy, *Code Name Mulberry* (David & Charles) 1977

HMSO Land at War: *The Official Story of British Farming 1939-44*, 1945

HMSO *Report of the Committee on Land Utilisation in Rural Areas* 1942

HMSO *Town and Country Planning Advisory Committee* 1938

Institution of Civil Engineers, *Civil Engineer in War* Vol. 2 1945

Leakey, J H., *School Errant* (The Queensgate Press) 1951

Rowland, Lucas, *The Voice of a Nation* (Gomer Press) 1981

Monnickendam, S. A., *Secrets of the Diamond* (Frederick Muller) 1941

Morgan, Dyfnallt, *Babi Sam* (BBC and the Gwynedd Archives Service) 1985

Murray, Keith A. H., *Agriculture* (HMSO and Longmans, Green & Co., London) 1955

Rowland, Peter, *David Lloyd George – a Biography* (Macmillan Publishing Co. Inc) 1975

Royal Aero Society Library *Conversion of American Aircraft* Saunders Roe Ltd.

Smith, David J., *Action Stations: Military Airfields of Wales and the North-West* (Patrick Stephens Ltd) 1981

Street, A. G., *Farmer's Glory* (Faber and Faber Ltd) 1932

Taylor, W J Crosland, *Crosville* (Transport Publishing Co. Ltd) 1948

Thomson, Malcolm, *David Lloyd George – the Official Biography* (Hutchinson), 1948.

Transactions of the Honourable Society of Cymmrodorion, *National Gallery 1945*

Wadsworth, John, *Counter Defensive* (Hodder & Stoughton) 1946

Williams, J Gwynn, *The University College of North Wales, 1884 - 1927* (Cardiff UWP) 1985

VJ Day Children's Street Party at Twthill, Caernarvon, 16 August 1945.
[Mrs Doris Rogers]